Fitness Running

Second Edition

Richard L. Brown, PhD
with Joe Henderson

Human Kinetics

W9-CBF-163

Library of Congress Cataloging-in-Publication Data

Brown, Richard L., 1937-
 Fitness running / Richard L. Brown ; with Joe Henderson.— 2nd ed.
  p.   cm.
  Includes index.
  ISBN 0-7360-4510-4 (soft cover)
  1. Running.   2. Physical fitness.   I. Henderson, Joe, 1943-   II. Title.
 GV1061 .B77 2003
 796.42—dc21

                                                                2002151052

ISBN: 0-7360-4510-4

Copyright © 2003 by Richard L. Brown and Joe Henderson
Copyright © 1994 by Human Kinetics Publishers, Inc.

All rights reserved. Except for use in a review, the reproduction or utilization of this work in any form or by any electronic, mechanical, or other means, now known or hereafter invented, including xerography, photocopying, and recording, and in any information storage and retrieval system, is forbidden without the written permission of the publisher.

Notice: Permission to reproduce the following material is granted to instructors and agencies who have purchased *Fitness Running, Second Edition:* page 80. The reproduction of other parts of this book is expressly forbidden by the above copyright notice. Persons or agencies who have not purchased *Fitness Running, Second Edition* may not reproduce any material.

Acquisitions Editor: Martin Barnard; **Developmental Editor:** Leigh LaHood; **Assistant Editor:** Alisha Jeddeloh; **Copyeditor:** Nancy Wallace Humes; **Proofreader:** Kim Thoren; **Indexer:** Betty Frizzéll; **Graphic Designer:** Nancy Rasmus; **Graphic Artist:** Sandra Meier; **Photo Manager:** Dan Wendt; **Cover Designer:** Keith Blomberg; **Photographer (cover):** Dan Wendt; **Photographer (interior):** photo on page 1 © Greg Crisp/SportsChrome USA; photo on page 41 © ImageState/Lindy Powers Studio; photo on page 81 © ImageState/Cheyenne Rouse Photography; all other photos by Dan Wendt, unless otherwise noted; **Printer:** Bang Printing

Human Kinetics books are available at special discounts for bulk purchase. Special editions or book excerpts can also be created to specification. For details, contact the Special Sales Manager at Human Kinetics.

Printed in the United States of America   10   9   8   7   6   5   4   3   2   1

Human Kinetics
Web site: www.HumanKinetics.com

United States: Human Kinetics
P.O. Box 5076, Champaign, IL 61825-5076
800-747-4457
e-mail: humank@hkusa.com

Canada: Human Kinetics
475 Devonshire Road Unit 100, Windsor, ON N8Y 2L5
800-465-7301 (in Canada only)
e-mail: orders@hkcanada.com

Europe: Human Kinetics
107 Bradford Road, Stanningley, Leeds LS28 6AT, United Kingdom
+44 (0) 113 255 5665
e-mail: hk@hkeurope.com

Australia: Human Kinetics
57A Price Avenue, Lower Mitcham, South Australia 5062
08 8277 1555
e-mail: liahka@senet.com.au

New Zealand: Human Kinetics
P.O. Box 105-231, Auckland Central
09-523-3462
e-mail: hkp@ihug.co.nz

Fitness Running

Contents

PART III
Scheduling Your Training

Preface

Nearly 10 years have raced past since Dick Brown and I last collaborated on the book *Fitness Running*. This revised edition is different from the first version because of all that has happened for Dick in the intervening decade.

During these years he coached Suzy Favor Hamilton and Vicki Huber onto the 1996 U.S. Olympic team. He led Marla Runyan into middle-distance running, which would take her to the 2000 Olympic 1500-meter final under another coach and then to the 2001 World Championships 5000, coached by yet another.

All of this is to be expected from Dick Brown. He has a long history of coaching world-class athletes, notably Mary Decker Slaney in her best years, which were topped by her two gold medals at the 1983 World Championships.

Dick is more than a running coach. He also has sent athletes to the Olympics in racewalking and cross-country skiing, as well as swimming in the Paralympics. Dick is more than a coach of world-beaters. The methods he prescribes for these athletes scale down well for use by runners of all levels. He's a scientist with an intimate understanding of what makes all exercising human beings work—and how they can work better. He combines scientific knowledge that few coaches can match with practical know-how that few physiologists can claim.

Dr. Dick has an inventive mind. He created the AquaJogger™, the most popular flotation device for deep-water training; and he holds a patent for the Individual Trainer, a handheld computer for calculating training efforts. For all these reasons he is an exercise expert who truly merits the title. His training plans continue to prove themselves even while he continues to improve them.

The progress of his programs make the second *Fitness Running* a different and better book than the one we wrote almost a decade ago. The cosmetic changes—moving from the somewhat rigid confines of a book series and dispensing with color-coded workouts—are the least of its differences. And we gave this book chapters on specific racing distances, though its title might imply (wrongly) that it offers *only* programs for reclaiming basic fitness.

The books, old and new, do outline a stay-in-shape program. But Dick pays particular attention to racers who run track distances of 1500 through 10,000 meters and on the roads from 5Ks to marathons. He offers runners a menu of workout options, varying widely in type and degree of difficulty. He then combines these choices into sensible training plans that can be tailored precisely to the runner's abilities and goals. These programs have changed substantially since the first book, because Dick's techniques have evolved.

The general principles that support these programs apply to all ages and abilities and to both sexes. Only the specifics of distance and pace vary for, say, a high school boy trying to qualify for his regional meet, a woman in her 30s trying to make the Olympic Trials, and a marathoner in middle age hoping to win a spot on the Boston starting line.

Decide your goal, then trust Dick Brown, who has helped runners reach the highest levels of the sport, to lead you wherever you want to run.

—Joe Henderson

Focusing on Running

You already know how to run. It's part of your ancestry and your upbringing.

Humans are a running species, and typical children are runners after their first steps. Few of us run right into adulthood, but we know the basic technique of putting one foot in front of the other at a faster-than-strolling pace.

So the question you want answered in this book isn't "How do I run?" It is "How can I run *better*?" The answer depends on who you are and what *better* means to you.

Let's say you ran track in high school, but that was many years and many pounds ago. The longer you've lapsed, the longer and more carefully you must work to get back into running shape. We'll show you the path to better basic fitness.

Perhaps you already run, but your daily 2 miles or 3 kilometers through the neighborhood aren't pleasant. You get hurt too often, or you feel physically or mentally flat much of the time. We'll show you better ways to train without strain.

Maybe you're running trouble-free, but you're looking for more from your activity. You see announcements for a local 5K (3.1-mile) race and wonder if you dare enter it. We'll show you how much more enjoyable running can be when you make it a social event.

Let's say that you have run a race and now want to go farther or faster. You aim to improve your personal record (PR) in the 5K, to go for a 10K (6.1-mile) next time, or to increase your distances all the way up to a marathon. We'll show you how to race better.

In this opening section of the book, we prepare you for your next step in running. We lay the groundwork for this progress by addressing and assessing basic requirements for all runners:

- Testing your physical readiness to start running or to adopt a more demanding training program (chapter 1)
- Selecting proper shoes, clothing, and other equipment to make your running more comfortable (chapter 2)
- Refining your running technique so that you can cover ground more smoothly and swiftly (chapter 3)
- Supplementing your running training with strength and flexibility exercises and cross-training activities (chapter 4)
- Staying healthy and safe as you train to become a fitter, faster, more enduring, and happier runner (chapter 5)

Assessing Your Running Level

Your first task, before launching into the running program that we prescribe, is to determine your starting point. In other words, just how healthy and fit are you? This question applies as much to experienced runners as to beginners.

The terms *health* and *fitness* aren't synonymous. Health is merely the absence of disease or injury. Fitness is the ability to perform a specific physical task. You can be healthy in the sense of being illness-free and uninjured but still unprepared for the performance demands of running. Or you can be fit from recent aerobic training but unhealthy in the medical sense.

Determine how healthy and fit you are by taking the two entrance exams in this chapter. Let the results tell you where to begin. Be honest with yourself here. If you ignore key items in your medical history or overestimate your capabilities, running will lead you to the painful truth. To minimize pain and maximize improvement, you must draw the starting line where it is right for you.

It's important to determine your level of fitness before embarking on a running program.

Test Your Health and Fitness

Here we ask you to assess honestly your health history and your fitness habits. Choose the number beside the statement that best describes you in each of the 10 important health and fitness factors. Add your total score in table 1.1 to determine how to start training for running.

1. **Cardiovascular health:** Which of these statements best describes your cardiovascular condition? This is a critical safety check before you enter any vigorous activity.

   (Warning: If you have a history of heart disease or if you are older than 35, enter a running program only after receiving clearance from your doctor and then with close supervision from a fitness instructor.)

   ❑ I have no history of problems. (3 points)
   ❑ Past ailments were treated successfully. (2 points)
   ❑ Such problems exist but need no treatment. (1 point)
   ❑ I am under medical care for cardiovascular illness. (0 points)

2. **Injuries:** Which of these statements best describes your current injuries? This is a test of your musculoskeletal readiness to start a running program.

   (Warning: If your injury is temporary, wait until it heals before starting the program. If the condition is chronic, adjust the program to fit your limitations.)

   ❑ I have no current injuries. (3 points)

   ❑ Current pain does not limit activity. (2 points)

   ❑ Current pain limits activity. (1 point)

   ❑ Ongoing pain prohibits strenuous training. (0 points)

3. **Illnesses:** Which of these statements best describes your current illnesses? Certain temporary or chronic conditions will delay or disrupt your running program. (See warnings under "Injuries.")

   ❑ I have no current illnesses. (3 points)

   ❑ Current illness does not limit activity. (2 points)

   ❑ Current illness limits activity. (1 point)

   ❑ Ongoing illness prohibits strenuous training. (0 points)

4. **Age:** Which of these age groups describes you? In general, the younger you are, the more likely you are to be in good physical shape.

   ❑ 19 years or younger (3 points)

   ❑ 20 to 29 years (2 points)

   ❑ 30 to 39 years (1 point)

   ❑ 40 or older (0 points)

5. **Weight:** Which of these statements describes how close you are to your own definition of ideal weight? Being overweight is a major mark of unfitness, but so is being significantly underweight.

   ❑ Within 5 pounds, or 2 kilograms, of ideal weight (3 points)

   ❑ Above or below by 6 to 10 pounds, or 3 to 4 kilograms, of ideal weight (2 points)

   ❑ Above or below by 11 to 19 pounds, or 5 to 8 kilograms, of ideal weight (1 point)

   ❑ Above or below by 20 or more pounds, or 9 kilograms, of ideal weight (0 points)

6. **Resting pulse rate:** Which of these statements describes your current pulse rate on waking up but before getting out of bed? A well-trained heart beats more slowly and efficiently than one that's less fit.

- ❏ Fewer than 60 beats per minute (3 points)
- ❏ 60 to 69 beats per minute (2 points)
- ❏ 70 to 79 beats per minute (1 point)
- ❏ 80 or more beats per minute (0 points)

7. **Smoking habits:** Which of these statements best describes your smoking history and current activity? Smoking is the number one enemy of health and fitness.
   - ❏ I have never smoked. (3 points)
   - ❏ I smoked but quit. (2 points)
   - ❏ I smoke occasionally. (1 point)
   - ❏ I smoke regularly. (0 points)

8. **Most recent run:** Which of these statements best describes your running within the past month? The best single measure of how well you will run in the near future is what you ran in the recent past.
   - ❏ I ran nonstop for more than 2 miles, or 3 kilometers. (3 points)
   - ❏ I ran nonstop for 1 to 2 miles, or 1.5 to 3 kilometers. (2 points)
   - ❏ I ran nonstop for less than 1 mile, or 1.5 kilometers. (1 point)
   - ❏ I have not run recently. (0 points)

9. **Running background:** Which of these statements best describes your running history? Running fitness isn't long-lasting, but the fact that you once ran is a good sign that you can do it again.
   - ❏ I ran regularly within the past year. (3 points)
   - ❏ I ran regularly one to two years ago. (2 points)
   - ❏ I ran regularly more than two years ago. (1 point)
   - ❏ I never ran regularly. (0 points)

10. **Related activities:** Which of these statements best describes your participation in other exercises that are similar to running in their aerobic benefit? The closer the activity relates to running (such as bicycling, swimming, cross-country skiing, and fast walking), the better the carryover effect.
    - ❏ I regularly practice similar aerobic activities. (3 points)
    - ❏ I regularly practice less-vigorous aerobic activities. (2 points)
    - ❏ I regularly practice nonaerobic activities. (1 point)
    - ❏ I am not regularly involved in physical activity. (0 points)

If you scored 20 points or more, you rate high in health and fitness for a beginning runner. You probably can handle continuous runs of 2 to 3 miles (3 to 5 kilometers), or 20 to 30 minutes.

At 10 to 19 points your score is average. You may need to take some walking breaks to complete runs of 2 to 3 miles (3 to 5 kilometers), or 20 to 30 minutes.

A score of less than 10 is low. You may need to start by walking, increasing the sessions to a half-hour before adding any running.

Table 1.1   Self-Analysis

Enter your scores from the health and fitness test in this chapter.

1. Cardiovascular health _____

2. Injuries   _____

3. Illnesses   _____

4. Age   _____

5. Weight   _____

6. Resting pulse rate   _____

7. Smoking habits   _____

8. Most recent run   _____

9. Running background   _____

10. Related activities   _____

          Total score _____

Test Your Running Fitness

Now comes your final exam, so to speak. This is the more telling test, because up to now you've surveyed your health and fitness only with pen and paper. Now you check it where it counts—on the run.

Kenneth Cooper, MD, the leading authority in aerobic fitness, has long recommended a 12-minute run (or run-walk mix). We advise you to do the same to see how much distance you can cover in this period. The results of this test match up well with those obtained from sophisticated laboratory findings. The key result here is your ability to take in and process the oxygen that fuels your running. Exercise scientists call this ability your maximal oxygen uptake and abbreviate it as $\dot{V}O_2max$. The volume (V) of oxygen (O_2) consumed by a person is expressed in milliliters per kilogram of body weight per minute of activity (ml/kg/min). Generally speaking, the more efficiently you transport and use oxygen, the faster you can run.

We use $\dot{V}O_2$max as a benchmark of fitness throughout this book. The farther you run in 12 minutes, the greater your oxygen-uptake reading. The less distance you cover within that time limit, the lower your reading. Take this test as follows:

1. Use a local track or a flat stretch of accurately measured road. The standard running track is 440 yards, or 400 meters. Four laps equal 1 mile, or 1.6 kilometers.
2. Start at a pace you can maintain throughout the 12 minutes.
3. Increase the pace slightly in the last 1 or 2 minutes.
4. Aim to feel tired but exhilarated at the finish, not exhausted.
5. Look forward to repeating this test in the future with excitement, not dread.

Grade yourself by the standards in table 1.2. The results place you in one of four running-fitness categories:

- Superior: 8 3/4 laps or more ($\dot{V}O_2$max of 60 and above)
- High: 7 1/2 to 8 1/2 laps ($\dot{V}O_2$max of 50 to 59)
- Average: 5 3/4 to 7 1/4 laps ($\dot{V}O_2$max of 35 to 49)
- Low: 5 1/2 laps or fewer ($\dot{V}O_2$max below 35)

If your score is low, don't be discouraged. Consider these two reasons: First, this test score is merely a starting point for your progress. The lower it is the more room you have for improvement in later tests. Second, this result gives you a realistic basis for selecting training programs in this book. The programs must be based on your current ability.

Table 1.2 12-Minute Test

Note that the 12-minute test also is used later in the book but with a different purpose than drawing a baseline of fitness. In chapter 6 you use this test to determine racing potential and training pace.

Laps	Miles (pace)	Kilometers (pace)	$\dot{V}O_2$max
LOW FITNESS			
3 3/4	0.94 (12:46)	1.5 (8:00)	22
4	1.00 (12:00)	1.6 (7:30)	24
4 1/4	1.06 (11:19)	1.7 (7:04)	25
4 1/2	1.13 (10:37)	1.8 (6:40)	27
4 3/4	1.19 (10:05)	1.9 (6:19)	29
5	1.25 (9:36)	2.0 (6:00)	31
5 1/4	1.31 (9:07)	2.1 (5:43)	33
5 1/2	1.38 (8:42)	2.2 (5:27)	35
AVERAGE FITNESS			
5 3/4	1.44 (8:20)	2.3 (5:13)	37
6	1.50 (8:00)	2.4 (5:00)	38
6 1/4	1.56 (7:42)	2.5 (4:48)	40
6 1/2	1.63 (7:22)	2.6 (4:37)	42
6 3/4	1.69 (7:06)	2.7 (4:27)	44
7	1.75 (6:51)	2.8 (4:17)	46
7 1/4	1.81 (6:38)	2.9 (4:08)	48
HIGH FITNESS			
7 1/2	1.88 (6:23)	3.0 (4:00)	50
7 3/4	1.94 (6:11)	3.1 (3:52)	52
8	2.00 (6:00)	3.2 (3:45)	54
8 1/4	2.06 (5:50)	3.3 (3:38)	56
8 1/2	2.13 (5:38)	3.4 (3:31)	58
SUPERIOR FITNESS			
8 3/4	2.19 (5:29)	3.5 (3:25)	60
9	2.25 (5:20)	3.6 (3:20)	62
9 1/4	2.31 (5:12)	3.7 (3:15)	64
9 1/2	2.38 (5:03)	3.8 (3:10)	66
9 3/4	2.44 (4:55)	3.9 (3:05)	68
10	2.50 (4:48)	4.0 (3:00)	70

Choosing
Shoes and Gear

Part of the beauty of running is its simplicity. What could be more basic than lacing up a good pair of running shoes, slipping into the right clothing for the conditions, and heading out your front door for a run?

Okay, maybe outfitting yourself for walking is even simpler. But your essential equipment purchases for running are few and relatively inexpensive compared with most other sports. In this chapter we advise you on what to purchase by way of shoes, clothing, and some of the more useful accessories that enhance running safety, comfort, accuracy, and enjoyment. You can, if so inclined, dress colorfully and stylishly for running. Or you can wear your old, baggy gray sweats.

You can spend hundreds of dollars on the newest high-tech shoes and the latest miracle fibers that both look great and feel great. Or you can make minimal, but still quite functional, purchases at a discount or secondhand store. Whether to dress up or down to run depends on your budget and fashion sense. We deal here only with the few essentials.

The list starts with shoes, and maybe it could end there. Even if you don't already run, your wardrobe probably holds all the clothes you need

© The PhotoNews

Running attire can range from matching pieces made specially for running to just the basic shorts and T-shirt.

to get you started. Almost any light, nonrestrictive clothing will work early in your training. But you can't run well in just any old shoes.

Your Shoes

You need shoes made specifically for running, because runners strike the ground with a force three or more times their body weight. The ground you strike is usually paved and unyielding, and running shoes are specially designed to absorb this shock.

High-quality running shoes feature several layers of cushioning on the sole, slight elevation of the heel, flexibility of the forefoot, and support against excessive side-to-side motion. All of this comes in a relatively lightweight package. Good shoes can be found in the $60 to $100 price range. You can buy look-alikes for less than $60, but they aren't bargains if they lack essential design features or durability. You can also pay more than $100, but you're probably spending money on an overdesigned shoe that won't noticeably improve your running. You're wise to stick with the established running-shoe makers. Running magazines deem these companies (listed alphabetically) worthy of inclusion in their annual shoe surveys. The most dependable brands are Adidas, Asics, Avia, Brooks, Diadora, Etonic, Fila, Mizuno, Montrail, New Balance, Nike, Puma, Reebok, Ryka, Salomon, and Saucony.

For specific shoe recommendations, check the buying guides in *Runner's World* magazine, *Running Times* magazine, and the Running Network. Then go to a running specialty store, where the staff is trained to help you make the right selection for your foot type (a flatter foot requires different shoe specifications than a foot with a high arch) and ensure proper fit. But you aren't finished just because you've bought the right shoes. You still need to deal with several aspects of shoe wear and care to enjoy trouble-free running.

- Shoe break-in. Even well-made running shoes require a break-in period. You should be able to put on a new pair and run without getting blisters, but any new shoes will cause your feet to hit the ground differently than they did in the old pair. You may develop soreness in your feet and legs while adapting to this change, so wear the new shoes only during easier runs until you've adapted.

- Shoe rotation. Each brand and model, and even each pair of the same model, cause slightly different stresses on the feet and legs. By rotating shoes, much as you would tires on a car, you even out these stresses. Buy two or more pairs of shoes, and switch off frequently.

- Shoe care. Well-used running shoes get dirty and stinky. They're made mostly of synthetic materials, and they can be washed. Hose them off frequently or throw them into the washer, but let them dry in the air instead of the dryer to prevent heat damage.

- Shoe wear. Running shoes commonly wear in two ways. The soles and heels not only grind down, of course, but also the cushioning materials on the sole fatigue and compress. You can repair the outer surfaces, but the shoe

© Greg Crisp/SportsChrome USA

Because of the force with which the foot strikes the ground, careful consideration should be given to shoe choice.

won't be much good if compression from use has changed the original shape and thickness of the sole. Most running shoes need to be replaced after 500 to 1,000 miles (800 to 1,600 kilometers) of wear.

• Shoe inserts. You can make a good shoe better by inserting protective devices. These include insoles to replace those in the shoe, upgraded arch supports, heel cushions, and custom-made shoe inserts called orthotics. The first three products are sold over the counter in sport and specialty stores, and the orthotic inserts are prescribed by a doctor. Use these devices only if you are troubled by injuries.

Your Clothing

Just as running shoes are designed to cushion your feet against hard, jarring surfaces, running clothing is made to keep you comfortable in weather extremes. (See chapter 5 for details about the effects of heat and cold on the runner.) Modern fabrics make running tolerable in all but the harshest conditions. Whether you outfit yourself from a specialty store or with items you already own, include the following in your running wardrobe:

• Underwear that supports without binding
• Socks that don't slide down and bunch up in your shoes (bunched-up socks can cause discomfort and blisters)
• Shorts that allow freedom of movement and don't chafe your inner thighs
• Shirts for different seasons—turtleneck, long-sleeved, short-sleeved, and sleeveless—in a variety of fabrics and weights
• Gloves or mittens to keep your hands warm (the hands get cold the quickest)
• Headwear for various weather conditions—a stocking hat for cold; a face mask (balaclava) for wind and cold; and a cap with a visor to shield out rain, sun, and blinding headlights
• Tights that protect against the cold and don't get baggy and heavy in the rain
• Sweatpants, windbreakers, and weatherproof suits—jacket and pants—to keep you comfortable in the worst conditions

Other Equipment

Your smallest piece of equipment is one of the most useful tools—a digital watch. This inexpensive piece of gear has a stopwatch feature that gives you instant, accurate information about your running pace. A higher-tech (and therefore more expensive) device, the heart-rate monitor, also provides feedback about your runs. It registers the level of effort that you're putting into a workout. And even a low-tech item like sunglasses has become a standard piece of equipment for many runners. The tinted lenses of the glasses reduce dangerous and annoying glare and perhaps prevent eye damage in bright sunlight.

If you prefer entertainment while running, take along a personal-listening device such as a CD or cassette player. Listen to it only when you run on a track or trail, away from traffic. If you run on the street, be warned that wearing headphones will tune in your music and tune out traffic noises, and that can be hazardous to your health.

Adding Up the Costs

How much you will spend on your running gear depends on how frugally or royally you wish to be outfitted. First we list the rock-bottom gear, then the high-end purchases. Your costs probably will fall between these low-end and high-end amounts.

Low-Budget Dressing

Limit your shopping list to a single item: shoes. Choose shoes made specifically for running from one of the major manufacturers listed in this chapter. Look for bargains among discontinued models and shoes discounted because of cosmetic defects. You should be able to find a pair for $60 or slightly less.

As for the other essentials, dress in clothing that you already own. Use the same wristwatch you now wear, provided it has a second hand or stopwatch feature.

High-Budget Dressing

Outfit yourself in style. Splurge on a waterproof, windproof suit and two pairs of high-quality shoes for different types of running (such as training and racing). Buy a runner's wristwatch that tells you everything except what to eat for breakfast.

Even the prices that follow aren't the highest you can go. You can duplicate other items besides shoes, and add accessories such as headphones, sunglasses, and a heart-rate monitor.

We're assuming that you already own suitable shorts, hats, gloves, socks, underwear, and T-shirts, but you can also find higher-end sports clothing specifically for runners—and it will show on the price tag. Here are a few you'll need and their cost:

Weatherproof suit: $200
Running shoes, two pairs: $200
Runner's watch: $100
Full-length tights: $50
Knee-length tights: $50
Total cost: $600

Checking Your Running Form

Running is as easy as putting one foot in front of the other, you might think. As long as you remember to alternate feet, you can't have too much trouble, right? Not quite. The act of running might be this simple if you were blessed with picture-perfect form, but very few of us are. And it wouldn't matter if your technique is ragged if the only time you run is to catch a bus. Truth is, you have bigger plans.

Small mistakes in the way you move can penalize you greatly as your distances grow longer and your speed picks up. To avoid wasting energy and time, you must pay attention to the details of your running form. Correct running form covers a wide range of personal differences, but four general rules apply to everyone:

1. The form must fit the individual. A small person, for instance, can't attempt the same stride length as someone a head taller.

2. The form must fit the pace. The faster you go, the more you run on your toes, lift your knees, and drive with your arms. The slower you

run, the lower and shorter the stride, and the less vigorous the arm action.

3. The form must be mechanically efficient. Humans are upright animals and run best that way—with a straight back and eyes looking forward, not down.

4. The form must be relaxed. Running with tension is like driving a car with its brakes on—it causes you to work harder but go slower.

How do you run? This isn't a question of how far, how fast, or how often. It's asking you to examine how you move. In this chapter, we look into the mechanics of sound running—from feet to head.

Feet First

Runners fall into two general categories: those who run *on* the ground and try to pound it flat, and those who run *over* the ground and use it as a springboard to stay airborne. Let the latter type serve as your model.

© Dennis Light/Light Photographic

Strive for spring in your running form.

Some runners can never sneak up behind you. Without looking over your shoulder, you can tell they're coming—clomp! clomp! clomp! You can almost feel their feet hit the ground. The noise indicates two related problems: overstriding (reaching out too far with the feet) and landing with the knees locked. Strive for silent running. This begins with a knee that is slightly flexed so that it can bend on impact. The foot then lands more directly under the body and at midfoot rather than heel first. As the ankle unlocks, you rock quickly back onto the heel, then forward again for liftoff (see figure 3.1). To put more spring in your run, check the foot, ankle, and knee.

a   b

Figure 3.1   Avoid *(a)* landing on the heel with the knee straight and ankle locked; correct foot action is to *(b)* land on the midfoot with knee slightly flexed and ankle unlocked.

- Foot. Make full use of it, from heel to midfoot to toes, as you roll through the running motion. Give a little push with the big toe as your foot leaves the ground.
- Ankle. Flex it. Use it to get more bounce. The more rigid the ankle is, the more jarring the contact with the ground will be.
- Knee. Lift it. The lift of the knee controls the ball of the foot. If the knee rides low and rigid, your foot will barely clear the ground. Pick up the knee and bend it.

Keep the word *prance* in mind as you perfect your foot-leg action. Run as if you're proud of yourself—quietly proud.

Fully Armed

You see both types. One runs like a boxer, trying to protect the face. The arms ride high and tight, the fists stop just short of the chin, and the shoulders are tense. The other runner dangles the arms at the sides with fingers pointed at the ground, as if these appendages served no useful purpose. In neither case do these arms and hands do these runners much good. In fact, the upper body plays important roles in two-legged locomotion. It counterbalances the action of the legs and provides driving force.

- Arm. The arm and leg swing in rhythm. The faster the beat, the more vigorously each arm moves. This accounts for the piston-like drive of sprinters. The action is more pendulum-like in distance running. The range of motion is smaller, and each arm swings somewhat across the chest but not past the midline.
- Hand. The hand controls the tension in your arm, as you can easily demonstrate to yourself. Hold out your hand, straighten the fingers, and notice the feeling of rigidity all the way up to your shoulder. Next, make a fist and clench it tightly. You're tense again. Now make a loose fist. Feel better? The unclenched fist, fingers resting lightly on the palm, promotes relaxed running.
- Wrist. As you move up the arm, check the wrist. It should be fixed in line with the arm so the hand is not left to flap aimlessly in the breeze.
- Elbow. Give careful attention to the elbow. It should always be unlocked. Otherwise, you sacrifice the driving and balancing potential of the arm. The arm gets its power from the up-and-down motion at elbow level. Try hammering a nail with a stiff elbow, then take advantage of the bend and notice how much more force you generate the second way. Similar forces are at work in running.
- Shoulder. The locked elbow also produces one of the most common form faults—a wasteful dipping and swaying motion of the shoulders. Ideally, the shoulder shows no apparent extraneous movement and both remain parallel to the running surface.

Figure 3.2, a-c, illustrates correct and incorrect upper-body form.

Heads Up

You've seen the runner who shuffles around the track with eyes fixed on the feet, and back and shoulders hunched forward in the shape of a number 9.

That's precisely how *not* to run. Straighten up. The best posture for a runner is erect, with the back perpendicular to the ground (see figure 3.3). The advantages are many: freer use of the legs through a greater range of motion, easier breathing as the unconstricted lungs fill more completely, and a view of something other than your feet.

Tell yourself to run tall! This means stretching up to your full height but short of running with the posture of a soldier at attention. Good posture begins just above the hips. Imagine the pelvis as a filled bowl, and try not

a

b

c

Figure 3.2 The arms should be neither *(a)* too high and tight nor *(b)* dangling low at the sides; they should be *(c)* at about a 90-degree angle, with hands in loose fists and elbows unlocked.

a   b

Figure 3.3 *(a)* Looking down at the feet causes hunched posture; *(b)* eyes should look straight ahead and posture should be upright.

to spill its contents by leaning forward too much. Keep your butt under your upper body.

The other key to proper posture is the head. The gaze of the eyes controls the lean of the body. Look forward, not downward. Cast your eyes to the horizon, or on a spot at least 10 steps ahead, and then everything else tends to fall into proper alignment.

Smooth, efficient running is also a product of muscle strength and flexibility. The next chapter deals with how to achieve these.

CHAPTER 4

Supplementing Your Training

What's the first image that comes to mind when you think of warm-up exercises? It's likely a picture of runners bending and stretching or perhaps leaning into walls or trees as if trying to push them over. Such exercises have become a standard in running training, and for good reasons. If they are done regularly and properly, they keep your stride fluid and reduce injuries. Don't, however, confuse these stretching exercises with warming up. They are two separate activities best done at opposite ends of the run. Warm up by running slowly, walking briskly, or mixing the two. Stretch after you run, either after this warm-up session or, more often, as part of the cool-down period after your run.

This chapter first discusses warming up and cooling down. Then we move to flexibility exercises, and finally to cross-training activities that substitute for or supplement running.

Warming to the Task

The best way to warm up before running is to start with a slow run or a fast walk. If you start by walking, move on to the slow run. Finally, slip into normal pace when your legs and lungs are ready for it.

Listen to your body, the running authorities advise. Run as you feel. Heed the body's messages to keep yourself fit and healthy. Listening, however, isn't always enough. You must know how to analyze and act on your body's signals and realize that the body sometimes tells lies. One of these times commonly is right before you start to run, and this is what makes the warm-up period so critical.

Let's say that you're an early-morning runner. You wake up stiff and tired in the chilly predawn. You think to yourself that you are in no shape to run and that your body is telling you to take a day off. Or perhaps you're a late-afternoon runner. A minor injury has interfered with your recent runs, but you don't notice it as you move through your day. You think you've recovered and are ready to resume running. Or could be you're facing a big race. Your anxiety has you feeling weak and doubtful. You believe you won't even have the strength to get to the starting line. In each of these scenarios, your body could be lying to you. If you believed everything it indicated before a run, you'd make a mistake on each of these three days. You might not have run on a morning that could have rejuvenated you. You might have ignored a minor injury that afternoon and made it major. Or you might have let prerace nerves erode your confidence.

Here's where the warm-up comes in. Besides warming you up physically, this phase

© ImageState/Tony Demin

Warming up, with a brisk walk for example, helps gauge the body's readiness to run on a certain day.

of your workout is a truth finder that motives you mentally. A warm-up tests your will and tells you whether you're able to run. It can ease aches that you thought were serious, or it can uncover those you tried to ignore, or it can chase away your doubts and fears.

It sometimes seems like the hardest part of running is getting started. Your mind and body rebel against taking the first steps. Ease into your run with the first steps of the warm-up.

Plan to walk or run easily for 10 to 20 minutes, roughly the first mile or two. You can integrate the warm-up into the mileage of a long, steady-pace run. Or you can separate it from a faster, timed session and perhaps insert some stretching exercises in between. (We give specific advice on this subject in chapter 7.)

By the time you've warmed up, your feelings will be telling the truth. Imaginary or transient problems will have eased if not vanished, and real concerns will still be there, if not intensified. After you've warmed up, listen closely to your body and believe what it says. Is it telling you to move on or to back off?

Easing Out of Activity

The cool-down phase is the warm-up in reverse, with one essential addition—stretching. Just as you warm up with fast walking and easy running to get ready for the harder running to come, you cool down with easy running and walking to shake off the effects of this work. You add stretching to the cool-down to thwart any negative physical effects from the run.

Your body is in overdrive when you finish running. The harder you ran, the higher your body's gear. You may be breathing hard and sweating heavily. At the least you're warm, your heart is beating at twice its normal rate, and your legs have taken a good pounding. The worst thing you can do to yourself now is jump into your car and drive home. Don't even sit down. Keep moving. Walk briskly or run easily for another 5 to 10 minutes, allowing your pulse and breathing rates to descend gradually toward normal.

Remember that the apparent air temperature rises about 20°F (nearly 10° C) while you're running. This will plummet again as soon as you stop and you'll feel chilly, so be prepared to exchange your sweat-soaked shirt for a dry one and to add extra clothing if you'll be outside for long. (Chapter 7 lists specific tips on cool-down activities.)

Stretching Out

Be aware that running is by its nature a tightening activity. It reduces the flexibility in the backs of your legs (particularly the calves and hamstrings).

If left uncorrected, this tightness sets you up for soreness and injury. Stretching counteracts the inflexibility that running causes, so it's best to stretch after you run, usually after the cool-down period.

Another good time to stretch is at the beginning of your workout as part of the warm-up and before a faster training session or race. Some runners also pause to stretch during long road races, such as a marathon, to work out their muscle tightness.

The muscles are most receptive to stretching when they're warm and tight, and they are least likely to be injured then by the very exercises that are supposed to prevent injury. Yes, you read that last line correctly. Stretching exercises can *cause* injuries if done improperly or at the wrong time. Because the running motion is quick and jarring, the therapeutic stretches must be slow and soothing. Remember to follow these three key rules of stretching:

1. Stretch slowly to the point of discomfort, but do not push or bounce into the pain zone.
2. Breathe normally—don't hold your breath.
3. Hold the exercise for several seconds at the borderline between comfort and discomfort.

The rest of this section outlines 10 ways to maintain and regain flexibility. These exercises are designed to counterbalance the tightening effects that running has on the muscles.

Plantar Arches

Kneel on all fours with your toes underneath you. Lower your buttocks backward and downward. Hold for 30 seconds.

Ankles (Sitting)

Sit with both legs extended, and cross your right leg over your left knee. Hold your right ankle or heel with your left hand and slowly pull your foot toward your body. Hold for 30 seconds. Repeat on the opposite leg.

Ankles (Standing)

Stand with your back flat against a wall or flat surface with your feet 1 or 2 feet in front of you. Turn your feet slightly inward and slowly lean forward, keeping your legs straight. Hold for 30 seconds.

Hamstrings

Sit with both legs extended. Bend your right leg and place the sole of your right foot against the inner side of your left thigh to form a 90-degree angle. Keep your left leg straight, bend at the waist, and slowly lower your upper body toward your thigh. Hold for 30 seconds. Repeat on the opposite leg.

Adductors

Sit with your legs straddled as much as possible. Keep your legs extended, bend at the waist, and lower your upper body toward your thigh. Hold for 30 seconds. Repeat on the opposite side.

Quadriceps

Stand with your right hand against a flat surface for balance and support. Bend your left leg behind you, grasping the foot with your left hand. Slightly flex your right leg and pull your left heel toward your buttocks. Be careful not to compress your knee joint too tightly. Hold for 30 seconds. Repeat with the opposite leg. Avoid this stretch if you have knee problems.

Buttocks and Hips

Stand with your hands at your sides. Cross your left leg behind your right leg. Turn to the right, bend at the waist, and try to touch the heel of your left leg with both hands, keeping your legs straight. Hold for 10 to 20 seconds. Repeat on the opposite side.

Lower Back

Lie flat on your back. Bend your knees toward your chest and grasp your hands behind your thighs. Pull your knees toward your chest and shoulders until your hips come off the ground. Hold for 10 to 20 seconds, then extend your legs slowly, one at a time.

Neck

Stand with both arms behind your back. Grasp your left elbow from behind with your right hand. Pull your elbow across the midline of your back, and tilt your head toward your right shoulder, keeping your left shoulder flat. Hold for 30 seconds. Repeat on the opposite side.

Shoulders

Stand and raise both arms over your head. Cross one wrist over the other and interlock your hands. Straighten your arms and stretch upward. Hold for 30 seconds.

Cross-Training

Running is one of many ways to get fit. We recommend that you mix fitness activities. Overspecialization can lead to physical injury and psychological staleness. Variety can spice up your routine.

We could write a separate book on the merits of multisport activity. But we'll limit our discussion to what cross-training offers runners who prefer to spend most of their training time running. An alternative workout serves three major purposes:

1. It offers another activity during injury periods. Most of the injuries that runners suffer will allow some type of exercise that won't aggravate the problem.

2. It provides mental breaks during times when the running routine has gone flat. Substituting another activity for a few days or weeks can restore the appetite to run.

3. It supplies rest-day activities. Runners rarely need pure rest on their days off, just a break from the jarring effects of running.

In all cases, cross-training provides active recovery. To accomplish this, supplemental workouts generally are low intensity and brief.

We think of the cross-trainer as a runner who indulges in similar activities such as swimming, bicycling, and walking. Two adjuncts to the runner's program don't quite fit our definition but nonetheless are too valuable not to mention in this context. One is stretching, which we discussed earlier. The other is strength building and balancing.

Strength Training

A complication is that the one-directional action of running builds some leg muscles more than others. Strength imbalances can occur, and these can lead to injuries. To maintain and restore muscle balance, we highly recommend that you add strength exercises to your program. These can be as simple as push-ups and sit-ups mixed into your stretching routine or as complex as a formal weight-training workout.

Other than stretching and strengthening, we encourage activities that mimic the aerobic nature of running. This is your true cross-training. Your choices are almost limitless. We highlight four activities that are the most comparable to running and most accessible to runners.

Floor and Water Aerobics

This is a favorite of people who like company when they exercise, because this is largely an organized group activity. Aerobics trains more muscle groups than running does, but beware of the high-impact exercises. They could hurt you or at least fail to provide adequate relief from the pounding nature of running. Opt for low-impact (on the floor) or no-impact (in the water) aerobics routines.

Road, Off-Road, and Stationary Bicycling

Runners like the road and mountain bike for many of the same reasons they like to run. Bicycling takes them outdoors on the same routes they would travel as runners and lets them explore twice as much territory as they could on foot. Stationary biking lacks these pluses, of course, but provides a low-impact workout. And it has the one great advantage over road biking (and road running, for that matter) of removing the threat of traffic and the rider's own carelessness.

Swimming

Unlike water running, you use the standard strokes here, preferably the crawl. The advantages of swimming over running (besides the obvious one of no impact) are that it exercises more of the body and at the same time promotes flexibility. But despite the great workout and lack of wear and tear, swimming is a solitary endeavor. Some runners, accustomed to looking around and talking with friends as they run, think of pool workouts as sensory deprivation.

Walking

This is the most available and least appreciated alternative. You can walk anywhere, anytime, and with very little risk of developing impact ailments. Walking delivers only about one-third the pounding of running. But because walking is such an efficient exercise, workouts tend to be low-intensity. The benefits are slower to come than they are with running and other cross-training activities, and you must walk a longer time to cover the same distance to achieve those benefits.

How Much Cross-Training?

We recommend limiting most of the recovery-type cross-training sessions to a half-hour so you won't drain energy from the next day's run. A half-hour's swim or bike ride is about equal in effort to a half-hour run—provided the intensity levels are the same.

The exception to this equal-time rule is walking. It will always be less intense than running and the other cross-training workouts, so you must walk about twice as long (or up to an hour on recovery days) to expend a similar amount of energy. Keep that amount small. The goal is to keep your cross-training refreshing, physically and emotionally.

CHAPTER 5

Monitoring Health and Fitness

Running can be healthy, but it isn't necessarily safe from physical consequences. Runners get hurt and sick—and in some cases, chronically sore and tired. Most of these conditions are self-caused—that is, they're a direct result of the activity itself and not some outside force or bad luck. If you bring on your own problems, you also can prevent them by monitoring your physical reactions to your running training. This chapter names the key warning signs.

Running teaches you what's going on inside yourself, and it gets you out of the house, the office, and the car. Outside is a great place to go most of the time. But you can't go safely and comfortably into the elements, natural and human-made, without preparations and precautions.

Weather, for instance, won't adapt to you. So you must learn how to cope with it—especially on the hottest and coldest days. This chapter advises you on how to prepare to run in extreme conditions.

Most runners train on roads for the practical reasons that roads are everywhere and available anytime. Running there puts you into competition with the greatest physical threat facing a runner—auto traffic. We offer tips on sharing road space safely.

Listening to Your Body

Successful training is a matter of applying and adapting to stress. Apply the right amount, and you adapt. Apply too much, and you set yourself up for poor performances, injuries, and illnesses.

Your body will tell you what work you can and can't handle, if you'll listen. The problem is that many active people don't want to take the time to listen or know how to respond.

By listening to what the body says and responding to its signals properly, you have a better chance of avoiding illness and injury, and maximizing performance. The most critical signals are heart rate, body weight, and hours of sleep.

If your heart rate is too high in the morning, you haven't recovered from the previous day's training, and your body is still struggling to rebuild. If your body weight goes down too fast, you haven't rehydrated. If you don't get the sleep you need, you're going to be in trouble, whether you're a world-class athlete or a recreational runner.

How can you tell if you're failing to adapt? By answering three simple questions each morning:

1. Was your resting pulse rate (taken before getting out of bed in the morning) 10 percent higher than normal?
2. Was your body weight (taken after voiding but before eating or drinking in the morning) 3 percent below normal in pounds or 1 1/2 percent below in kilograms?
3. Was your sleep last night 10 percent less than normal?

If you answer *no* to all these questions, go ahead with your planned training. If you answer *yes* to one question, be prepared to cut short the day's workout.

If you answer *yes* to two questions, plan to run at an easy pace. If you answer *yes* to all three, take the day off. And when in doubt, be conservative!

Creating a Positive Climate

The weather during running isn't what it appears to be as you prepare to run. Don't believe only what you see as you look out the window, and don't base your running comfort level on what the thermometer says.

Winter days won't seem as cold once you start your run. Summer days won't feel as perfect as they did when you set out. That's because a 20°

Fahrenheit (F) rule works to either warm up a runner on a cold day or make the heat feel unbearable on a hot day. The apparent Fahrenheit temperature will climb by that amount as you hit your stride. In Celsius (C), it's about a 10° difference.

For example, a chilly 40°F (5°C) morning will feel like a pleasant 60°F (15°C). A balmy 75°F (24°C) afternoon will become an unpleasant 95°F (34°C). Your body has a good furnace but a bad air conditioner. It warms up nicely in cold weather but cools down poorly on hot days.

Plan your runs with the 20°F (10°C) rule in mind. Dress for how the temperature will feel in midrun, not how it feels at the starting line. Dress in layers that can be stripped away as you warm up—jacket, long-sleeved shirt, T-shirt, long pants, tights, cap, and gloves.

Run in the cooler hours of a summer day. Save your hardest runs for the coolest days (perhaps those with rain, or wind, or clouds). In winter, reverse this pattern. Run during the warmer hours, and run hardest on the warmest days (when the sun is out, the wind is calm, and the snow has melted off the roads).

Don't let summer heat or winter cold keep you indoors. A well-dressed runner can train safely in any season. But you still must consider the potential risks at either temperature extreme. Hot days carry the possibility of heat exhaustion and cold days the risk of frostbite. Again, the temperature on the thermometer may not reveal the whole truth. High humidity makes hot days feel hotter than the actual temperature because your body can't cool as efficiently. And high wind makes cold days colder. Plan your

© The PhotoNews

In cold weather, run during the warmer hours of the day.

running and your wardrobe according to the heat-humidity readings in table 5.1 and windchill readings in table 5.2.

Table 5.1   Hot-Weather Ratings

Find the temperature down the left side of the scale and the humidity level across the top. Go to the point where these two figures meet for the day's letter grade. An "A" day is the best for running, and an "F" is the worst. Temperatures below 70°F (22°C), down to where they start feeling cold, rate "A" grades, and those above 95°F (35°C) are graded "F" at all humidity levels.

TEMPERATURE	HUMIDITY LEVEL (PERCENT)								
	20	30	40	50	60	70	80	90	100
70°F/22°C	A	A	A	A	A	A	A	B	B
75°F/24°C	A	A	A	A	A	B	B	B	C
80°F/26°C	A	A	B	B	B	B	C	C	C
85°F/29°C	B	B	C	C	C	D	D	D	F
90°F/32°C	C	C	D	D	D	F	F	F	F
95°F/35°C	D	D	F	F	F	F	F	F	F

Table 5.2   Cold-Weather Ratings

Find the wind speed down the left side of the scale and the temperature across the top. Go to the point where these two readings meet for the day's letter grade. An "A" day is the best for running, and an "F" is the worst. Temperatures above 35°F (1°C) all rate "A" grades, and those below –10°F (–19°C) are graded "F" at most wind speeds.

WIND READING					TEMPERATURE				
Fahrenheit	35°	30°	25°	20°	15°	10°	5°	0°	–5°	–10°
Celsius	1°	–1°	–3°	–6°	–8°	–10°	–12°	–15°	–17°	–19°
Calm	A	A	A	B	B	B	C	C	C	D
5 mph (2 mps)	A	A	B	B	B	C	C	C	D	D
10 mph (5 mps)	A	B	B	B	C	C	C	D	D	D
15 mph (7 mps)	B	B	B	C	C	C	D	D	D	F
20 mph (9 mps)	B	B	C	C	C	D	D	D	F	F
25 mph (11 mps)	B	C	C	C	D	D	D	F	F	F
30 mph (13 mps)	C	C	C	D	D	D	F	F	F	F
35 mph (15 mps)	C	C	D	D	D	F	F	F	F	F
40 mph (17 mps)	C	D	D	D	F	F	F	F	F	F

Individuals differ, of course, in their reactions to heat and cold. You also adapt somewhat as you train in these conditions and then learn how you dress for them.

Generally speaking, however, we can rate these conditions by how they affect your running. We've taken National Weather Service readings for heat-humidity and windchill, and given them letter grades:

A = good day

B = fair day

C = marginal day

D = poor day

F = unsafe day

Following the Rules of Road Running

Special tracks or trails are nice bonuses, but they aren't a requirement for running. Anywhere you may walk can become a running course. This often means taking to the roads. For your protection, follow these rules:

- Choose roads with sidewalks or wide shoulders as your safety zone, and run on the left side to face oncoming traffic.

- Yield the right of way, and assume that the road belongs to the cars (as well as trucks, motorcycles, and even bicycles), if only because of their size and speed.

- Treat drivers courteously, and never provoke them by invading their lanes, dashing in front of them, or berating them after close calls.

- Anticipate drivers' moves by doing the thinking for them, and make eye contact with them at risky crossings.

- Stay alert by keeping your head up and eyes on the road, and fight the tendency to daydream the miles away and ignore road conditions.

- Wear brightly colored clothing during the daytime, and put on reflective items at night to make yourself more visible.

- Hear what's coming, and leave your CD player and other distractions at home so you can stay more aware of dangers.

Not all threats on the streets and roads are vehicular. They also can be human. Runners, especially women, can become targets of belligerent and predatory individuals. To protect yourself, follow the rules listed previously, run in places and at times that pose minimum risk, and stay alert to threats.

Planning Your Program

Challenge is necessary for improvement, but the challenges must not exceed the body's ability to handle them. We call this approach *CBS*—challenging but safe.

For example, Mary Slaney had trouble when she ran above a certain training load. But when I tried to restrain her, she would plead, "Dick, I'm not training hard enough."

Armed with her past training results, I'd say, "Mary, last year at this time you were doing a lot of work, and this set the limit of your race pace then. Now you're doing more and should be able to run faster." This assessment calmed her down and gave her the health and confidence to win the 1500- and 3000-meter races at the 1983 World Championships.

The training programs in this book aren't reserved for the elite. They are equally applicable to the elderly and the young, male and female, beginners and veterans. All worthwhile aerobic training programs—whether for casual exercise running or for serious competitive training—address three basic questions: How long? How hard? How often? The basic fitness formula can be expressed as the acronym FIT. It stands for frequency (how often you train), intensity (how hard you train), and time (how long you train). You must train often enough, hard enough, and long enough to stimulate the improvements you're seeking. Yet you must balance the work with recovery; otherwise you risk exhaustion or injury, which could halt your progress. All training is a balancing act between "enough" and "too much."

Training needs also vary according to the individual runner's ability and immediate goal. Keeping these facts in mind, we offer specific guidelines for tailoring training to your needs.

- Chapter 6 provides details on setting up a highly personalized program.
- Chapter 7 gives a menu of workout options and instructions on completing those sessions.
- Chapter 8 tells you how to write your own book, a log of your training, and racing plans and results.

CHAPTER

6

Program Setup

It is fitting that this part of the book is the second of three, because the book centers on this part. It tells exactly how to plan your workouts.

At the heart of part II sits this chapter, and at the heart of the heart is the concept of $\dot{V}O_2$max. This is shorthand for volume of oxygen consumed at maximal aerobic effort (also known as *maximal oxygen uptake*). $\dot{V}O_2$max is a vital indicator of endurance fitness. Because it underlies all the workouts and training schedules in this book, we give an extended example of how it works.

An inactive but healthy adult might have a $\dot{V}O_2$max of about 31 milliliters per kilogram per minute (ml/kg/min), which would enable that person to run a mile in about 9:00. An excellent runner may have a $\dot{V}O_2$max of about 75, which would allow that person to run a mile in about 4:10.

If both of these people weigh 154 pounds (70 kilograms), the inactive one would use 19,530 milliliters of oxygen during the mile run. The superfit runner will use 22,052 milliliters. If we look at these amounts another way, a soft-drink can holds 355 milliliters. The sedentary person used 55 cans of oxygen in the mile, although the skilled runner used 62 in less than half the time.

Your $\dot{V}O_2$max reading is one of the most reliable ways to gauge your capacity for endurance activity. This isn't a fixed figure, because it changes with your fitness level. You need to know your current reading to determine the amount and pace of training that you can handle right now.

Find Your $\dot{V}O_2$max

You can estimate this figure three ways: by predicting what you can run now, by calculating this figure from a recent (within the past month) race result, or by finding the distance you can cover in a 12-minute run/walk. Here are the steps necessary to determine your $\dot{V}O_2$max reading each of these ways.

Determining $\dot{V}O_2$max by predicting times

1. Select one to five racing distances from table 6.1 (for example, mile, 5K, 10K).
2. Predict the times you know you can now run for these distances, and be conservative (for example, mile, 5:45; 5K, 20:30; 10K, 44:15).
3. Look up in table 6.1 the $\dot{V}O_2$max number closest to, but below, those times (for example, mile, 52; 5K, 50; 10K, 48).
4. Find the $\dot{V}O_2$max numbers for each distance. If there are more than one, add them up, and divide by the number of events (for example, from step 3: 150 ÷ 3 = 50).
5. Go to the number closest to but below this solution on the $\dot{V}O_2$max line (for example, 50).

Use this $\dot{V}O_2$max number for setting up your training program.

Determining $\dot{V}O_2$max from a recent race

1. Select from table 6.1 the distance you raced within the past month (for example, 5K).
2. List the time you ran in that race (for example, 20:27).
3. Look up in table 6.1 the $\dot{V}O_2$max number closest to, but below, that time (for example, 50).

Use this $\dot{V}O_2$max number for setting up your training program.

Determining $\dot{V}O_2$max from a 12-minute test

1. Select a trail, road, or track with a distance you can determine.
2. Start running or walking at a pace you can maintain for 12 minutes. Run continuously, walk continuously, or alternate running and walking.

Table 6.1   Determining V̇O₂max From a Race

Locate the time nearest to, but slower than, your actual result from a race within the past month. Or estimate your current racing ability at this distance. Then find the corresponding $\dot{V}O_2$max. For example, a 5K of 20:27 equates to a $\dot{V}O_2$max reading of 50.

$\dot{V}O_2$max	Mile/ 1500 meters	5K	10K	Half- marathon	Marathon
22	12:48/11:55	42:16	1:27:50	3:14:25	7:11:34
24	11:49/11:01	39:09	1:21:22	3:00:03	6:40:08
26	10:59/10:14	38:30	1:15:51	2:47:46	6:13:15
28	10:16/9:34	34:12	1:11:04	2:37:09	5:49:58
30	9:38/8:58	32:11	1:08:53	2:27:52	5:29:36
32	9:05/8:28	30:25	1:03:12	2:19:41	5:11:37
34	8:35/8:00	28:50	59:55	2:12:24	4:55:37
36	8:09/7:36	27:26	59:59	2:05:54	4:41:18
38	7:45/7:13	26:09	54:20	2:00:02	4:28:23
40	7:24/6:54	25:00	51:57	1:54:43	4:16:41
42	7:05/6:36	23:57	49:46	1:49:53	4:06:02
44	6:47/6:19	23:00	47:46	1:45:28	3:56:17
46	6:31/6:04	22:07	45:56	1:41:25	3:47:19
48	6:16/5:50	21:18	44:15	1:37:40	3:39:04
50	6:02/5:37	20:33	42:42	1:34:13	3:31:26
52	5:49/5:25	19:51	41:15	1:31:01	3:24:21
54	5:37/5:14	19:13	39:54	1:28:02	3:17:45
56	5:26/5:03	18:36	38:39	1:25:15	3:11:36
58	5:16/4:54	18:02	37:28	1:22:39	3:08:51
60	5:06/4:45	17:31	36:22	1:20:13	3:00:27
62	4:57/4:36	17:01	35:20	1:17:56	2:55:23
64	4:49/4:29	16:33	34:22	1:15:47	2:50:36
66	4:41/4:22	16:06	33:27	1:13:45	2:46:06
68	4:33/4:14	15:41	32:35	1:11:50	2:41:51
70	4:26/4:07	15:18	31:46	1:10:01	2:37:50

3. With about 2 minutes remaining, pick up the pace if you are able. Finish feeling tired but exhilarated, not exhausted.

4. Calculate the distance you covered in 12 minutes (for example, 1.87 miles, or 3.02 kilometers).

5. Look up in table 6.2 the $\dot{V}O_2$max number closest to, but below, that distance (for example, 50).

Use this $\dot{V}O_2$max number for setting up your training program.

Choose a Training Purpose

How you train will depend on what you want to accomplish. Decide which of these two levels of running most closely fits your interests and abilities:

1. Training for fitness
2. Training to race

If you plan to run/walk for fitness, skip to the "Choose Your Training Program" section of these instructions. Otherwise, go to "Choose a Race Goal."

Choose a Race Goal

How you train, and for how long, will depend on your chosen racing distance. This book offers programs at five different events, 1 mile or 1500 meters through marathon.

1. Select a distance for which you want to train and the training period for that distance: 1 mile or 1500 meters, 13 weeks; 5K, 13 weeks; 10K, 15 weeks; half-marathon, 18 weeks; marathon, 26 weeks (for example, 13 weeks for 5K).

2. Count the number of weeks back from the race date, and start your program on the preceding Sunday. For example, race date is June 8, so the 13-week program begins on March 10.

3. Select a goal time four $\dot{V}O_2$max points higher than your current $\dot{V}O_2$max number in table 6.1. For example, current $\dot{V}O_2$max is 50; current race time is near 20:33. Goal $\dot{V}O_2$max is 54; goal race time would be near 19:13.

4. Use a $\dot{V}O_2$max four points higher when the program calls for *goal pace* (for example, 54, or 6:11 per mile [3:50 per kilometer] for a 5K of about 19:13).

Table 6.2   Finding $\dot{V}O_2$max From a 12-Minute Test

Run, run/walk, or walk for 12 minutes on a track or an accurately measured route, and check the distance covered in that time. One lap of a standard track is 440 yards (1/4 mile) or 400 meters (0.4 kilometer). For example, 7.6 laps on a track is 1.87 miles, or 3.02 kilometers, for a $\dot{V}O_2$max of about 50.

$\dot{V}O_2$max	Miles	Kilometers	Laps
22	0.94	1.52	3.8
24	1.01	1.63	4.1
26	1.08	1.74	4.4
28	1.15	1.85	4.6
30	1.22	1.97	4.9
32	1.29	2.08	5.2
34	1.36	2.19	5.5
36	1.42	2.29	5.7
38	1.49	2.40	6.0
40	1.55	2.49	6.2
42	1.62	2.60	6.5
44	1.68	2.70	6.8
46	1.75	2.81	7.0
48	1.81	2.91	7.3
50	1.87	3.02	7.6
52	1.94	3.12	7.8
54	2.00	3.22	8.1
56	2.06	3.31	8.3
58	2.12	3.41	8.5
60	2.18	3.50	8.8
62	2.24	3.60	9.0
64	2.30	3.70	9.3
66	2.37	3.81	9.5
68	2.43	3.91	9.8
70	2.48	4.00	10.0

Choose a Long-Run Duration

Longer-than-normal runs figure prominently in the training programs of this book. Answer this question: If today were day 1 of your training program, what is the maximum number of minutes you could run/walk in a single training session—and safely do the same number of minutes on day 3? Be conservative (for example, 60 minutes).

20 minutes

30 minutes

40 minutes

50 minutes

60 minutes

70 minutes

80 minutes

90 minutes

100 minutes

110 minutes

120 minutes

Determine the length of shorter runs based on your current maximum length. See table 6.3 for runs that are one-fourth, one-half, and two-thirds of maximum. For example, one-fourth of the 60-minute maximum is 15 minutes; one-half of maximum is 30 minutes; two-thirds of maximum is 40 minutes.

Table 6.3   Determining Run Duration

Estimate the longest time you could now run, and repeat this same workout two days later. Based on that maximum, here are fractions of that time period. For example, if you can run 60 minutes, your typical easy recovery run would last a half-hour.

Max time	One-fourth max	One-half max	Two-thirds max
20 min	5 min	10 min	14 min
30 min	8 min	15 min	20 min
40 min	10 min	20 min	27 min
50 min	13 min	25 min	34 min
60 min	15 min	30 min	40 min
70 min	18 min	35 min	47 min
80 min	20 min	40 min	54 min
90 min	23 min	45 min	60 min

Now determine the pace you run in a particular period. Divide the time in minutes by the distance in miles or kilometers. For example, 6.2 miles (10 kilometers) in 60 minutes = 9:40 per mile (6:00 per kilometer).

Choose Your Running Intensity

Your effort will vary widely, depending on the intent of the day's workout. The four main effort levels used in this book are based on percentages of your $\dot{V}O_2$max and are defined as such:

Easy: 50% to 60% of $\dot{V}O_2$max

Moderate: 60% to 70% of $\dot{V}O_2$max

Somewhat strong (SWS): 75% to 85% of $\dot{V}O_2$max

Strong: 90% to 110% of $\dot{V}O_2$max

The 110 percent is not a misprint. Certain *strong* efforts exceed your $\dot{V}O_2$max and take you, briefly, into oxygen debt.

Table 6.4 lists paces at various effort levels, according to your $\dot{V}O_2$max. At some fitness levels, *easy* might mean walking, and *moderate* might mean mixing running with walking breaks. The table for *strong* efforts gives paces for distances less than a mile (1600 meters), which you use for interval, speed, and race-preparation workouts.

For example, $\dot{V}O_2$max of 50 equates to *easy* efforts of 10:03 to 12:04 per mile (6:12 to 7:30 per kilometer), *moderate* efforts of 8:37 to 10:03 per mile (5:20 to 6:12 per kilometer), *somewhat strong* efforts of 7:06 to 8:03 per mile (4:24 to 4:58 per kilometer), *strong* efforts of 5:29 to 6:42 per mile (3:24 to 4:09 per kilometer).

Table 6.4   Finding Training Intensity

Using your $\dot{V}O_2$max readings, select your proper training pace at the various levels of effort: *easy, moderate, somewhat strong,* and *strong.* The tables include a pace range per mile and per kilometer. A table for *strong* efforts gives paces for 100 to 800 meters. For example, a strong pace for a runner with a $\dot{V}O_2$max of 50 is 5:29 to 6:42 per mile, or 3:24 to 4:09 per kilometer.

EASY RANGE (MILE/KILOMETER)

$\dot{V}O_2$max	50% $\dot{V}O_2$max	60% $\dot{V}O_2$max
22	25:36 mile/15:55 km	21:20 mile/13:12 km
24	23:38 mile/14:37 km	19:42 mile/12:13 km
26	21:58 mile/13:38 km	18:18 mile/11:20 km
28	20:31 mile/12:42 km	17:06 mile/10:36 km

(continued)

(continued)

EASY RANGE (MILE/KILOMETER)

$\dot{V}O_2$max	50% $\dot{V}O_2$max	60% $\dot{V}O_2$max
30	19:16 mile/12:00 km	16:03 mile/9:55 km
32	18:10 mile/11:17 km	15:05 mile/9:22 km
34	17:11 mile/10:40 km	14:19 mile/8:52 km
36	16:18 mile/10:06 km	13:35 mile/8:26 km
38	15:31 mile/9:36 km	12:56 mile/8:00 km
40	14:48 mile/9:00 km	12:20 mile/7:37 km
42	14:09 mile/8:45 km	11:48 mile/7:19 km
44	13:34 mile/8:26 km	11:18 mile/7:00 km
46	13:01 mile/8:04 km	10:51 mile/6:42 km
48	12:32 mile/8:22 km	10:26 mile/6:27 km
50	12:04 mile/7:30 km	10:03 mile/6:12 km
52	11:38 mile/7:12 km	9:42 mile/6:01 km
54	11:15 mile/6:57 km	9:22 mile/5:50 km
56	10:53 mile/6:45 km	9:04 mile/5:39 km
58	10:32 mile/6:30 km	8:47 mile/5:28 km
60	10:13 mile/6:19 km	8:31 mile/5:16 km
62	9:54 mile/6:10 km	8:15 mile/5:05 km
64	9:37 mile/5:57 km	8:01 mile/4:58 km
66	9:21 mile/5:46 km	7:48 mile/4:50 km
68	9:06 mile/5:38 km	7:35 mile/4:42 km
70	8:52 mile/5:31 km	7:23 mile/4:35 km

MODERATE RANGE (MILE/KILOMETER)

$\dot{V}O_2$max	60% $\dot{V}O_2$max	70% $\dot{V}O_2$max
22	21:20 mile/13:12 km	18:17 mile/11:20 km
24	19:42 mile/12:09 km	16:53 mile/10:28 km
26	18:18 mile/11:20 km	15:41 mile/9:44 km
28	17:06 mile/10:36 km	14:40 mile/9:06 km
30	16:03 mile/9:55 km	13:46 mile/8:34 km
32	15:08 mile/9:22 km	12:58 mile/8:04 km
34	14:19 mile/8:52 km	12:16 mile/7:37 km
36	13:35 mile/8:26 km	11:39 mile/7:11 km
38	12:56 mile/8:00 km	11:05 mile/6:53 km
40	12:20 mile/7:38 km	10:34 mile/6:34 km
42	11:48 mile/7:19 km	10:07 mile/6:16 km

MODERATE RANGE (MILE/KILOMETER)

$\dot{V}O_2$max	60% $\dot{V}O_2$max	70% $\dot{V}O_2$max
44	11:18 mile/7:00 km	9:41 mile/6:00 km
46	10:51 mile/6:42 km	9:18 mile/5:46 km
48	10:26 mile/6:27 km	8:57 mile/5:31 km
50	10:03 mile/6:12 km	8:37 mile/5:20 km
52	9:42 mile/6:01 km	8:19 mile/5:09 km
54	9:22 mile/5:50 km	8:02 mile/5:00 km
56	9:04 mile/5:38 km	7:46 mile/4:50 km
58	8:47 mile/5:28 km	7:31 mile/4:39 km
60	8:31 mile/5:16 km	7:18 mile/4:31 km
62	8:15 mile/5:05 km	7:05 mile/4:24 km
64	8:01 mile/4:58 km	6:52 mile/4:17 km
66	7:48 mile/4:50 km	6:41 mile/4:09 km
68	7:35 mile/4:42 km	6:30 mile/4:02 km
70	7:23 mile/4:35 km	6:20 mile/3:54 km

SOMEWHAT STRONG RANGE (MILE/KILOMETER)

$\dot{V}O_2$max	75% $\dot{V}O_2$max	85% $\dot{V}O_2$max
22	17:04 mile/10:36 km	15:45 mile/9:44 km
24	15:45 mile/9:46 km	13:54 mile/8:37 km
26	14:39 mile/9:03 km	12:55 mile/8:00 km
28	13:41 mile/8:30 km	12:04 mile/7:30 km
30	12:51 mile/7:45 km	11:20 mile/7:00 km
32	12:06 mile/7:30 km	10:41 mile/6:38 km
34	11:27 mile/7:04 km	10:06 mile/6:16 km
36	10:52 mile/6:45 km	9:35 mile/5:57 km
38	10:21 mile/6:23 km	9:08 mile/5:34 km
40	9:52 mile/6:08 km	8:42 mile/5:24 km
42	9:26 mile/5:50 km	8:20 mile/5:09 km
44	9:03 mile/5:36 km	7:59 mile/4:58 km
46	8:41 mile/5:24 km	7:40 mile/4:47 km
48	8:21 mile/5:11 km	7:22 mile/4:31 km
50	8:03 mile/4:58 km	7:06 mile/4:24 km
52	7:46 mile/4:50 km	6:51 mile/4:15 km
54	7:30 mile/4:39 km	6:37 mile/4:06 km
56	7:15 mile/4:30 km	6:24 mile/3:58 km

(continued)

(continued)

SOMEWHAT STRONG RANGE (MILE/KILOMETER)

$\dot{V}O_2$max	50% $\dot{V}O_2$max	60% $\dot{V}O_2$max
58	7:01 mile/4:20 km	6:12 mile/3:50 km
60	6:48 mile/4:13 km	6:00 mile/3:43 km
62	6:36 mile/4:06 km	5:50 mile/3:36 km
64	6:25 mile/3:58 km	5:40 mile/3:30 km
66	6:14 mile/3:50 km	5:30 mile/3:24 km
68	6:04 mile/3:45 km	5:21 mile/3:17 km
70	5:55 mile/3:39 km	5:13 mile/3:13 km

STRONG RANGE (MILE/KILOMETER)

$\dot{V}O_2$max	90% $\dot{V}O_2$max	110% $\dot{V}O_2$max
22	14:13 mile/8:48 km	11:38 mile/7:12 km
24	13:08 mile/8:07 km	10:45 mile/6:40 km
26	12:12 mile/7:34 km	9:59 mile/6:12 km
28	11:24 mile/7:04 km	9:20 mile/5:46 km
30	10:42 mile/6:38 km	8:45 mile/5:24 km
32	10:05 mile/6:15 km	8:15 mile/5:07 km
34	9:33 mile/5:54 km	7:49 mile/4:50 km
36	9:03 mile/5:36 km	7:25 mile/4:35 km
38	8:37 mile/5:20 km	7:03 mile/4:20 km
40	8:13 mile/5:05 km	6:44 mile/4:09 km
42	7:52 mile/4:54 km	6:26 mile/3:59 km
44	7:32 mile/4:39 km	6:10 mile/3:51 km
46	7:14 mile/4:28 km	5:56 mile/3:40 km
48	6:58 mile/4:20 km	5:42 mile/3:32 km
50	6:42 mile/4:09 km	5:29 mile/3:24 km
52	6:26 mile/3:58 km	5:17 mile/3:17 km
54	6:15 mile/3:51 km	5:07 mile/3:10 km
56	6:03 mile/3:45 km	4:57 mile/3:04 km
58	5:51 mile/3:37 km	4:47 mile/2:59 km
60	5:40 mile/3:32 km	4:38 mile/2:51 km
62	5:30 mile/3:25 km	4:30 mile/2:46 km
64	5:21 mile/3:19 km	4:22 mile/2:40 km
66	5:12 mile/3:13 km	4:15 mile/2:36 km
68	5:03 mile/3:06 km	4:08 mile/2:32 km
70	4:56 mile/3:02 km	4:02 mile/2:29 km

STRONG RANGE (100 TO 800 METERS)

$\dot{V}O_2$max		100 m	150 m	200 m	300 m	400 m	800 m
22	90%	:51	1:27	1:43	2:35	3:28	7:00
	110%	:42	1:03	1:24	2:07	2:50	5:44
24	90%	:47	1:21	1:35	2:23	3:12	6:28
	110%	:38	1:00	1:28	1:57	2:37	5:17
26	90%	:44	1:06	1:28	2:13	2:58	6:01
	110%	:36	:52	1:12	1:49	2:26	4:55
28	90%	:41	1:01	1:22	2:04	2:47	5:37
	110%	:33	:50	1:07	1:42	2:16	4:36
30	90%	:38	:58	1:17	1:57	2:37	5:16
	110%	:31	:47	1:03	1:36	2:08	4:19
32	90%	:36	:54	1:13	1:50	2:28	4:58
	110%	:30	:45	1:00	1:30	2:01	4:04
34	90%	:34	:51	1:09	1:44	2:20	4:42
	110%	:28	:42	:56	1:25	1:54	3:51
36	90%	:32	:49	1:06	1:39	2:12	4:28
	110%	:27	:40	:54	1:21	1:48	3:39
38	90%	:31	:47	1:02	1:34	2:06	4:15
	110%	:25	:38	:51	1:17	1:43	3:38
40	90%	:29	:44	:59	1:30	2:00	4:03
	110%	:24	:36	:49	1:13	1:38	3:19
42	90%	:28	:42	:57	1:26	1:55	3:52
	110%	:23	:35	:47	1:10	1:34	3:10
44	90%	:27	:41	:55	1:22	1:50	3:43
	110%	:22	:34	:45	1:07	1:30	3:02
46	90%	:26	:39	:52	1:19	1:46	3:34
	110%	:21	:32	:43	1:05	1:27	2:55
48	90%	:25	:37	:50	1:16	1:42	3:26
	110%	:20	:30	:41	1:02	1:23	2:48
50	90%	:24	:36	:48	1:13	1:38	3:18
	110%	:20	:30	:40	1:00	1:20	2:42
52	90%	:23	:35	:47	1:11	1:35	3:11
	110%	:19	:28	:38	:58	1:17	2:36
54	90%	:22	:34	:45	1:08	1:31	3:05
	110%	:18	:27	:37	:56	1:15	2:31

(continued)

(continued)

STRONG RANGE (100 TO 800 METERS)

$\dot{V}O_2$max		100 m	150 m	200 m	300 m	400 m	800 m
56	90%	:22	:33	:44	1:06	1:28	2:59
	110%	:18	:27	:36	:54	1:12	2:26
58	90%	:21	:30	:42	1:04	1:26	2:53
	110%	:17	:26	:35	:52	1:10	2:21
60	90%	:20	:30	:41	1:02	1:23	2:48
	110%	:17	:25	:34	:51	1:08	2:17
62	90%	:20	:30	:40	1:00	1:21	2:43
	110%	:16	:24	:33	:49	1:06	2:13
64	90%	:19	:28	:39	:58	1:18	2:38
	110%	:16	:23	:32	:48	1:04	2:09
66	90%	:19	:28	:38	:57	1:16	2:34
	110%	:15	:22	:31	:46	1:02	2:06
68	90%	:18	:27	:37	:55	1:14	2:29
	110%	:15	:22	:30	:45	1:01	2:02
70	90%	:18	:27	:36	:54	1:12	2:26
	110%	:14	:21	:29	:44	:59	1:59

Choose Your Training Program

You're now ready to find the program that fits your current goal, based on answers to the previous questions. Fill in table 6.5 with the specifics of your training. See chapter 8 for detailed instructions on individual workouts, and see the following chapters for day-to-day programs:

Chapter 9: Beginning Training

Chapter 10: Fitness Training

Chapter 11: Recovery Training

Chapter 12: Short-Race Training

Chapter 13: Half-Marathon Training

Chapter 14: Marathon Training

Table 6.5   Planning Your Training Program

Following the instructions in this chapter, fill in the answers that apply to your current running and immediate goals. Incorporate this information into your training program.

1. What is your $\dot{V}O_2$max?

   From predicted race results:

   Distances and times _____

   Average $\dot{V}O_2$max _____

   From a recent race result:

   Distance _____

   Time _____

   $\dot{V}O_2$max _____

   From a 12-minute run/walk:

   Distance covered _____

   $\dot{V}O_2$max _____

2. What is your training purpose?

   Training for fitness _____

   Training to race _____

3. What is your race goal? (If you don't plan to race, skip to question 4.)

   Race distance _____

   Length of training program _____

   Race date _____

   Start-of-training date _____

   Goal time for the race _____

   Training pace (per mile/km) _____

   Goal pace (per mile/km) _____

4. What is your long-run duration?

   Current maximum time   _____   (distance) _____

   Two-thirds of maximum time   _____   (distance) _____

   One-half of maximum time   _____   (distance) _____

   One-fourth of maximum time   _____   (distance) _____

(continued)

Table 6.5   *(continued)*

5. What is your training intensity (pace per mile or per kilometer)?

Easy range	50% _____	60% _____
Moderate range	60% _____	70% _____
Somewhat strong range	75% _____	85% _____
Strong range (mile/km)	90% _____	110% _____
Strong range (100-800 meters)		
100 m	90% _____	110% _____
150 m	90% _____	110% _____
200 m	90% _____	110% _____
300 m	90% _____	110% _____
400 m	90% _____	110% _____
800 m	90% _____	110% _____

Do you feel overwhelmed by numbers? We've asked you to do considerable calculating in this chapter, but it's necessary and valuable for individualizing your training. Realize that the numbers represent the framework to construct your personal training program.

Workout Ingredients

We take a cookbook approach to running training in the remainder of this book. In cooking you achieve satisfying results by combining quality ingredients in proven recipes. The same is true here, though this book offers more flexibility in combining ingredients than most cookbooks do.

First we familiarize you with the ingredients by describing them completely in this chapter. Then we give you recipes for successful running in part III.

The raw materials are the individual workouts. The full list appears in table 7.4. Descriptions and instructions follow, moving from the slowest and easiest sessions to the fastest and hardest. When in doubt in training and racing, be conservative—except in the last half of your goal race; then, if in doubt, be aggressive.

Note that workouts are given priority numbers in this chapter and throughout part III. The most important session of the week is priority one, the least important is priority seven. If you are planning only to run four days a week, you should schedule priorities one, two, three, and four.

Before moving to the workouts, here is a brief lesson to figure out how far and fast you run.

Determining Distance and Pace

Most Americans train by mile distances, but competitive running is an increasingly metric sport. So this is a *bilingual* book, quoting distances by both miles and kilometers.

One kilometer (commonly referred to as K) equals 1000 meters, or 62 percent of a mile. One mile is 1609 meters, a 5-mile run is 8.05 kilometers, and 10 miles is 16.1 kilometers. The marathon equals 26.22 miles, or 42.19 kilometers.

Table 7.1 lists yard/mile equivalents for various standard training and racing distances. Table 7.2 shows both pace-per-mile and per-kilometer for the most commonly run distances.

Standard outdoor running tracks measure either 400 meters or 1/4 mile (440 yards) per lap. The difference in metric and yard lap times amounts only to fractions of a second, so we use only metric distances for track workouts. Table 7.3 gives training pace for distances of 800 meters and less.

Table 7.1   Metric and Mile Conversions

These two lists help translate commonly run distances from meters to miles, and vice versa.

Metric distance	Yard/mile equivalent
50 m	54.68 yards
100 m	109.36 yards
150 m	164.04 yards
200 m	218.72 yards
300 m	328.08 yards
400 m	437.44 yards
500 m	526.81 yards
600 m	656.17 yards
800 m	874.88 yards
1000 m	1,093.61 yards
1200 m	1,312.33 yards
1500 m (1.5K)	.93 mile (1620.42 yards)
1600 m	.99 mile

Metric distance	Yard/mile equivalent
3000 m (3K)	1.86 miles
3200 m	1.98 miles
5000 m (5K)	3.11 miles
8000 m (8K)	4.97 miles
10,000 m (10K)	6.21 miles
12 km	7.46 miles
15 km	9.32 miles
20 km	12.43 miles
Half-marathon (21.1K)	13.11 miles
25 km	15.54 miles
30 km	18.64 miles
Marathon (42.2K)	26.22 miles

Yard/mile distance	Metric equivalent
50 yards	45.72 m
100 yards	91.44 m
110 yards	100.58 m
150 yards	137.16 m
220 yards (1/8 mile)	201.67 m
330 yards	301.64 m
440 yards (1/4 mile)	402.34 m
550 yards	502.92 m
660 yards (3/8 mile)	603.50 m
880 yards (1/2 mile)	804.67 m
1,100 yards (5/8 mile)	1006.34 m
1,320 yards (3/4 mile)	1207.01 m
1 mile	1609 m (1.61K)
2 miles	3218 m (3.22K)
5 miles	8.01 km
10 miles	16.09 km
Half-marathon (13.1 miles)	21.10 km
20 miles	32.18 km
Marathon (26.2 miles)	42.19 km

Table 7.2   Finding Per-Mile/Kilometer Pace

Times at longer distances make more sense when you break them down into pace-per-mile or per-kilometer terms. This table assists with those conversions at five racing distances.

Mile/ kilometer	1500 meters	5K	10K	Half- marathon	Marathon
4:00/2:28	3:43				
4:10/2:35	3:53	12:56			
4:20/2:42	4:02	13:27	26:54		
4:30/2:48	4:11	13:58	27:56		
4:40/2:54	4:21	14:29	28:58	1:01:11	
4:50/3:00	4:30	15:00	30:00	1:03:22	2:07:44
5:00/3:06	4:40	15:30	31:00	1:05:33	2:11:06
5:10/3:13	4:49	16:01	32:02	1:07:44	2:15:28
5:20/3:19	4:58	16:32	33:04	1:09:55	2:19:50
5:30/3:25	5:07	17:03	34:06	1:12:06	2:24:12
5:40/3:31	5:17	17:34	35:08	1:14:17	2:28:34
5:50/3:38	5:26	18:05	36:10	1:16:28	2:32:56
6:00/3:44	5:36	18:36	37:12	1:18:40	2:37:19
6:10/3:50	5:45	19:07	38:14	1:20:51	2:41:41
6:20/3:56	5:54	19:38	39:16	1:23:02	2:46:03
6:30/4:02	6:03	20:09	40:18	1:25:13	2:50:12
6:40/4:09	6:12	20:40	41:20	1:27:24	2:54:47
6:50/4:15	6:21	21:11	42:22	1:29:35	2:59:09
7:00/4:21	6:31	21:42	43:24	1:31:47	3:03:33
7:10/4:27	6:40	22:13	44:26	1:33:28	3:07:55
7:20/4:33	6:49	22:44	45:28	1:36:09	3:12:17
7:30/4:40	6:59	23:15	46:30	1:38:20	3:16:39
7:40/4:46	7:08	23:46	47:32	1:40:31	3:21:01
7:50/4:52	8:08	24:17	48:34	1:42:42	3:25:23
8:00/4:58	7:27	24:48	49:36	1:44:53	3:29:45
8:10/5:05	7:36	25:19	50:38	1:47:04	3:34:07
8:20/5:11	7:45	25:50	51:40	1:49:15	3:38:29
8:30/5:17	7:55	26:21	52:42	1:51:26	3:42:51
8:40/5:23	8:04	26:52	53:44	1:53:37	3:47:13
8:50/5:29	8:14	27:23	54:46	1:50:48	3:51:35
9:00/5:36	8:23	27:54	55:48	1:58:00	3:56:00
9:10/5:42	8:33	28:25	56:50	2:00:11	4:00:22

Mile/ kilometer	1500 meters	5K	10K	Half-marathon	Marathon
9:20/5:48	8:42	28:56	57:52	2:02:22	4:04:44
9:30/5:54	8:52	29:27	58:54	2:04:33	4:09:06
9:40/6:00	9:01	29:58	59:56	2:06:44	4:09:06
9:50/6:06	9:11	30:29	1:00:58	2:08:55	4:17:50
10:00/6:12	9:20	31:00	1:02:00	2:11:00	4:22:00
10:10/6:18	9:29	31:31	1:03:02	2:13:11	4:26:22
10:20/6:24	9:38	32:02	1:04:04	2:15:22	4:30:44
10:30/6:30	9:47	32:33	1:05:06	2:17:33	4:35:06
10:40/6:36	9:56	33:04	1:06:08	2:19:44	4:39:28
10:50/6:42	10:06	33:35	1:07:10	2:21:55	4:44:50
11:00/6:49	10:15	34:06	1:08:12	2:24:06	4:48:12
11:10/6:55	10:24	34:37	1:09:14	2:26:18	4:52:36
11:20/7:01	10:33	35:08	1:10:16	2:28:29	4:56:58
11:30/7:07	10:43	35:39	1:11:18	2:30:40	5:01:20
11:40/7:13	10:52	36:10	1:12:20	2:32:21	5:04:42
11:50/7:20	11:02	36:41	1:13:22	2:34:32	5:09:04
12:00/7:27	11:11	37:12	1:14:24	2:36:44	5:13:26
12:10/7:33	11:20	37:43	1:15:26	2:38:55	5:17:48
12:20/7:39	11:30	38:14	1:16:28	2:41:06	5:22:10
12:30/7:45	11:39	38:45	1:17:30	2:43:17	5:26:32
12:40/7:51	11:48	39:16	1:18:32	2:45:28	5:30:54
12:50/7:57	11:58	39:47	1:19:34	2:47:39	5:35:18
13:00/8:04	12:07	40:18	1:20:36	2:49:50	5:39:40
13:10/8:10	12:16	40:49	1:21:38	2:52:01	5:44:02
13:20/8:16	12:26	41:20	1:22:40	2:54:12	5:48:24
13:30/8:22	12:35	41:51	1:23:42	2:56:23	5:52:46
13:40/8:28	12:44	42:22	1:24:44	2:58:34	5:57:08
13:50/8:34	12:54	42:53	1:25:46	3:00:45	6:01:30
14:00/8:41	13:03	43:24	1:26:48	3:02:56	6:05:52
14:10/8:47	13:12	43:55	1:27:50	3:05:07	6:10:14
14:20/8:53	13:22	44:26	1:28:52	3:07:18	6:14:36
14:30/8:59	12:31	44:57	1:29:54	3:09:29	6:18:58
14:40/9:05	12:40	45:28	1:30:56	3:11:40	6:23:20
14:50/9:11	12:50	45:59	1:31:58	3:13:51	6:27:42

Table 7.3   Figuring Training Pace (100 to 800 meters)

Interval and speed sessions employ distances less than a mile. Here are the splits that equate to various per-mile and per-kilometer paces.

Mile/kilometer	100 m	150 m	200 m	300 m	400 m	800 m
4:00/2:28	:15	:23	:30	:45	1:00	2:00
4:10/2:35	:15	:24	:31	:46	1:02	2:05
4:20/2:42	:16	:25	:32	:48	1:05	2:10
4:30/2:48	:16	:26	:33	:50	1:07	2:15
4:40/2:54	:17	:27	:35	:52	1:10	2:20
4:50/3:00	:18	:27	:36	:54	1:12	2:25
5:00/3:06	:18	:28	:37	:56	1:15	2:30
5:10/3:13	:19	:29	:38	:58	1:17	2:35
5:20/3:19	:20	:30	:40	1:00	1:20	2:40
5:30/3:25	:20	:31	:41	1:01	1:22	2:45
5:40/3:31	:21	:32	:42	1:03	1:25	2:50
5:50/3:38	:21	:33	:43	1:05	1:27	2:55
6:00/3:44	:22	:34	:45	1:07	1:30	3:00
6:10/3:50	:23	:35	:46	1:09	1:32	3:05
6:20/3:56	:23	:36	:47	1:10	1:35	3:10
6:30/4:02	:24	:37	:48	1:12	1:37	3:15
6:40/4:09	:25	:38	:50	1:15	1:40	3:20
6:50/4:15	:26	:38	:51	1:17	1:42	3:25
7:00/4:21	:26	:39	:52	1:19	1:45	3:30
7:10/4:27	:26	:40	:53	1:20	1:47	3:35
7:20/4:33	:27	:41	:55	1:22	1:50	3:40
7:30/4:40	:28	:42	:56	1:24	1:52	3:45
7:40/4:46	:28	:43	:57	1:26	1:55	3:50
7:50/4:52	:29	:44	:58	1:28	1:57	3:55
8:00/4:58	:30	:45	1:00	1:30	2:00	4:00
8:10/5:05	:30	:46	1:01	1:31	2:03	4:05
8:20/5:11	:31	:47	1:02	1:33	2:06	4:10
8:30/5:17	:31	:48	1:03	1:35	2:07	4:15
8:40/5:23	:32	:49	1:05	1:37	2:10	4:20
8:50/5:29	:33	:49	1:06	1:39	2:12	4:25
9:00/5:36	:33	:50	1:07	1:41	2:15	4:30
9:10/5:42	:34	:51	1:08	1:43	2:17	4:35
9:20/5:48	:35	:52	1:10	1:45	2:20	4:40
9:30/5:54	:35	:53	1:11	1:47	2:22	4:45

Mile/kilometer	100 m	150 m	200 m	300 m	400 m	800 m
9:40/6:00	:36	:54	1:12	1:48	2:25	4:50
9:50/6:06	:36	:55	1:13	1:50	2:27	4:55
10:00/6:12	:37	:56	1:15	1:53	2:30	5:00
10:10/6:18	:38	:57	1:16	1:55	2:32	5:05
10:20/6:24	:39	:58	1:18	1:57	2:35	5:10
10:30/6:30	:39	:59	1:19	1:58	2:37	5:15
10:40/6:36	:40	1:00	1:20	2:00	2:40	5:20
10:50/6:42	:40	1:01	1:21	2:02	2:42	5:25
11:00/6:49	:41	1:02	1:23	2:04	2:45	5:30
11:10/6:55	:42	1:03	1:24	2:06	2:47	5:35
11:20/7:01	:42	1:04	1:25	2:07	2:50	5:40
11:30/7:07	:43	1:05	1:26	2:09	2:52	5:45
11:40/7:13	:44	1:06	1:28	2:12	2:55	5:50
11:50/7:20	:45	1:07	1:29	2:14	2:57	5:55

Workout Options

We use just eight workout categories in this book (see table 7.4). However, within these groupings the sessions are infinitely variable in length and pace to fit a runner's abilities and ambitions.

Chapter 6 contains tables for determining your $\dot{V}O_2$max. Your *max time* is how far you can run in minutes and still be able to repeat the same

Table 7.4   Menu of Workouts

This list summarizes your eight choices. See details on pages 65 to 72. (SWS pace means somewhat strong.)

Workout run	Pace	% $\dot{V}O_2$max	Time/distance
Recovery	Easy	50-60%	1/4 to 1/2 max time
Long	Moderate	60-70%	Max-plus time
Steady state	SWS	75-85%	2/3 max-plus time
Tempo	SWS to strong	85-95%	1/2 max time
Interval	Strong	90-110%	200 m, 300 m, 400 m
Speed	Strong	90-110%	100 m, 150 m
Race preparation	Goal pace	100%	800 m, mile, 2 miles
Race	Goal pace	100%	Mile to marathon

workout two days later. (For instance, maybe you ran 2 hours, but could you safely and enjoyably do it again within 48 hours?) The programs in part III tell exactly how many minutes to add in *max-plus* runs.

Fast repetition runs (interval, speed, and race preparation) are followed by recovery jog/walks of equal distance to the runs. Most workouts contain additional warm-up and cool-down periods. See details on pages 65 to 72.

Use the workout ingredients to customize a program that fits your own fitness and scheduling needs.

Recovery Runs

Description: These are the easiest training days of the week, other than rest days. But that doesn't mean they're unimportant. Recovery days, like rest, help the body prepare for harder days. The pace is easy and the distances are relatively short on recovery days. You can mix running and walking, or even mix brief runs into what is mostly a walk.

Priority: Low, with a rating five, six, or seven (priority one being the most important, seven the least). Note that these runs are first to be replaced by rest or alternative-training days.

Duration: One-fourth to one-half of current maximum running time or distance

Pace or effort: Easy

Percentage of $\dot{V}O_2$max: 50 to 60 percent. See tables in chapter 6 to calculate your $\dot{V}O_2$-based pace.

Warm-up: Nothing formal, except possibly a 5-minute walk before starting to run. Otherwise treat the first 5 to 10 minutes as a warm-up by running at slower-than-normal pace.

Cool-down: Possibly a 5-minute walk and then stretching exercises.

Typical workouts:

For a fitness runner with a 36 $\dot{V}O_2$max and a max-time run of 30 minutes—15 minutes at 13:35 to 16:18 per mile (8:26 to 10:06 per kilometer)

For a mile to 10K runner with a 50 $\dot{V}O_2$max and max-time run of 60 minutes—30 minutes at 10:03 to 12:04 per mile (6:12 to 7:30 per kilometer)

For a half-marathon to marathon runner with a 50 $\dot{V}O_2$max and a max-time run of 90 minutes—45 minutes at 10:03 to 12:04 per mile (6:15 to 7:30 per kilometer)

Long Runs

Description: *Long* is in the eye of the beholder, meaning it's at least one-third longer than what you normally run. These runs begin to build an endurance base in fitness runners and firm up that base in competitive runners. For the fitness runner it also makes the normal runs seem a little shorter. For the half-marathoner and marathoner it is a rehearsal of what they'll run on race day. For fitness runners walk breaks are an acceptable option during long runs.

Priority: High, always a rating of one (priority one being the most important, seven the least) unless the week includes a second long run, which rates a two.

Duration: Current maximum time or distance, plus additional minutes as assigned in each program's weekly schedule. Runs do not exceed 120 minutes (two hours), except in rare cases for marathoners.

Pace or effort: Moderate

Percentage of $\dot{V}O_2$max: 60 to 70 percent. See tables in chapter 6 to calculate your $\dot{V}O_2$-based pace. As the run progresses and you feel good, you can pick up the pace during the last half of the distance.

Warm-up: Nothing formal, except possibly a 5-minute walk before starting to run. Otherwise treat the first 5 to 10 minutes as a warm-up by running at slower-than-normal pace.

Cool-down: Possibly a 5-minute walk and then stretching exercises.

Typical workouts:

For a fitness runner with a 36 $\dot{V}O_2$max and a max-time run of 30 minutes—30 minutes at 11:39 to 13:35 per mile (7:11 to 8:26 per kilometer)

For a mile to 10K runner with a 50 $\dot{V}O_2$max and max-time run of 60 minutes—60 minutes at 8:37 to 10:03 per mile (5:20 to 6:12 per kilometer)

For a half-marathon to marathon runner with a 50 $\dot{V}O_2$max and a max-time run of 90 minutes—90 minutes at 8:37 to 10:03 per mile (5:20 to 6:12 per kilometer)

Steady-State Runs

Description: Now the pace picks up as you transition between the slower-paced workouts that preceded this one and the higher-speed training that follows. You push the pace noticeably more than on recovery runs but cover about one-third less distance than in the long runs. This is the workout where you learn to run your most efficient training pace, which gives the most return for your effort.

Priority: High to medium, with a rating of one, two, or three (priority one being the most important, seven the least), depending on the week and program. Note that many weeks include two or even three steady-state runs.

Duration: Two-thirds of current maximum time or distance, plus additional minutes as assigned in each program's weekly schedule. Added time ranges from 1 to 10 minutes.

Pace or effort: Somewhat strong

Percentage of $\dot{V}O_2$max: 75 to 85 percent. See tables in chapter 6 to calculate your $\dot{V}O_2$-based pace.

Warm-up: Run easily or walk for 5 to 10 minutes.

Cool-down: Run easily or walk for 5 to 10 minutes and then stretch.

Typical workouts:

For a fitness runner with a 36 $\dot{V}O_2$max and a max-time run of 30 minutes— 20 minutes at 9:35 to 10:52 per mile (5:57 to 6:45 per kilometer)

For a mile to 10K runner with a 50 $\dot{V}O_2$max and max-time run of 60 minutes—40 minutes at 7:06 to 8:03 per mile (4:24 to 4:58 per kilometer)

For a half-marathon to marathon runner with a 50 $\dot{V}O_2$max and a max-time run of 90 minutes—60 minutes at 7:06 to 8:03 per mile (4:24 to 4:58 per kilometer)

Tempo Runs

Description: *Tempo* is another word for *pace*. All runs have tempo, you might say, but here the word takes on a special meaning. In tempo runs you travel at close to your race pace but for a shorter-than-racing distance. A thorough warm-up is essential for this workout, and its faster time helps your body adapt to the demands of racing.

Priority: High, with a rating of one or two (priority one being the most important, seven the least). Note that tempo runs usually replace long runs for those weeks.

Duration: One-half of current maximum time or distance. The actual length is shorter for track racers than for marathoners.

Pace or effort: Somewhat strong to strong

Percentage of $\dot{V}O_2$max: 85 to 95 percent. See tables in chapter 6 to calculate your $\dot{V}O_2$-based pace.

Warm-up: Run easily or run-walk for 5 to 10 minutes, then 4×50-meter strides (at about the pace of the day's tempo run, with 50-meter recovery jog/walks) and then stretching exercises.

Cool-down: Repeat warm-up but without the strides.

Typical workouts:

For a fitness runner with a 36 $\dot{V}O_2$max and a max-time run of 30 minutes—15 minutes at 8:15 to 9:35 per mile (5:07 to 5:57 per kilometer)

For a mile to 10K runner with a 50 $\dot{V}O_2$max and max-time run of 60 minutes—40 minutes at 6:05 to 7:06 per mile (3:47 to 4:24 per kilometer)

For a half-marathon to marathon runner with a 50 $\dot{V}O_2$max and a max-time run of 90 minutes—60 minutes at 6:05 to 7:06 per mile (3:47 to 4:24 per kilometer)

Interval Runs

Description: This repetition training alternates fast and slow segments. These are your most structured workouts, usually on a track and for specified distances with recovery periods of the same length in between. You run at race pace or slightly above. The intensity prepares you for a strong finish in a race.

Priority: High to medium, with a rating of one, two, three, or four (priority one being the most important, seven the least), depending on the week and program. Note that most interval workouts are twos and threes.

Duration: 200, 300, or 400 meters (220, 330, or 440 yards). Number of repeats varies by length, week, and program. Recovery jog/walks between intervals are equal length.

Pace or effort: Strong

Percentage of $\dot{V}O_2$max: 90 to 110 percent. See tables in chapter 6 to calculate your $\dot{V}O_2$-based pace.

Warm-up: Run easily or run-walk for 5 to 10 minutes, then $4 \times$ 50-meter strides (at about the pace of the day's interval runs, with 50-meter recovery jog/walks) and then stretching exercises.

Cool-down: Repeat warm-up but without the strides.

Typical workouts:

For a fitness runner—no interval workouts scheduled in this book

For a mile runner with a 50 $\dot{V}O_2$max—5 $\times$ 300 meters in 1:00 to 1:13 each

For a 5K to 10K runner with a 50 $\dot{V}O_2$max—10 $\times$ 400 meters in 1:20 to 1:38 each

For a half-marathon to marathon runner with a 50 $\dot{V}O_2$max—12 $\times$ 400 meters in 1:20 to 1:38 each

Speed Runs

Description: Note that you're allowed here—even encouraged—to run up to 110 percent of $\dot{V}O_2$max. That means you briefly exceed your maximum aerobic capacity. The speed runs don't last longer than 150 meters. They teach acceleration and faster leg turnover, which are especially valuable at ends of races, and also make the overall race pace seem a little slower.

Priority: Medium, with a rating of three or four (priority one being the most important, seven the least).

Duration: 100 or 150 meters (110 or 165 yards). Number of repeats varies by length, week, and program. Recovery jog/walks between speed runs are equal length.

Pace or effort: Strong

Percentage of $\dot{V}O_2$max: 90 to 110 percent. See tables in chapter 6 to calculate your $\dot{V}O_2$-based pace.

Warm-up: Run easily or run-walk for 5 to 10 minutes, then 4×50-meter strides (at about the pace of the day's speed run, with 50-meter recovery jog/walks) and then stretching exercises.

Cool-down: Repeat of warm-up but without the strides.

Typical workouts:

For a fitness runner—no speed workouts scheduled in this book

For a mile to 10K runner, or a half-marathon to marathon runner with a 50 $\dot{V}O_2$max—12×100 meters in 20 to 24 seconds each

Race-Preparation Runs

Description: These training runs are most like racing itself. You run at goal pace, defined in this book as a $\dot{V}O_2$max four points higher than your level when you began this program. The emphasis is on repetitions that are longer than you've run in previous workouts and faster than your interval runs.

Priority: High to medium, with a rating of one, two, or three (priority one being the most important, seven the least), depending on the week and program. Note that some weeks include two race preps.

Duration: 400 and 800 meters (440 and 880 yards), 1 mile and 2 miles (1600 and 3200 meters). Number of repeats varies by length, week, and program. Recovery jog/walks between race-prep runs are equal length.

Pace or effort: Goal pace, four points higher than $\dot{V}O_2$max at beginning of program

Percentage of $\dot{V}O_2$max: 100 percent. See tables in chapter 6 to calculate your $\dot{V}O_2$-based pace.

Warm-up: Run easily or run-walk for 5 to 10 minutes, then 4×50-meter strides (at about the pace of the day's race-prep runs, with 50-meter recovery jog/walks) and then stretching exercises.

Cool-down: Repeat of warm-up but without the strides.

Typical workouts:

For a fitness runner—no race-preparation workouts scheduled in this book

For a mile to 10K runner with a beginning $\dot{V}O_2$max of 50 and a goal-pace $\dot{V}O_2$max of 54—5×800 meters in 2:31 to 3:05 each

For a half-marathon to marathon runner with a beginning $\dot{V}O_2$max of 50 and a goal-pace $\dot{V}O_2$max of 54—5×1 mile in 6:37 to 7:30 each

Running the Race

Description: This is what you've been aiming for all along—the *big day*. Training will have told you by now if you're ready to reach goal pace or not. We hope you are. Races less important than the target event might also be part of your buildup and replace some of the week's tempo runs.

Priority: Highest, a definite rating of one—not only for that week but for the entire program. Note that all training tapers off for at least a week before the target race.

Duration: Distance for which you've trained in recent weeks and months—mile/1500, 5K, 10K, half-marathon, or marathon.

Pace or effort: Goal pace, four points higher than $\dot{V}O_2$max at beginning of program

Percentage of $\dot{V}O_2$max: 100 percent

Warm-up: Run easily or run-walk for 5 to 10 minutes, then 4×50-meter strides (at about the pace of the day's tempo run, with 50-meter recovery jog/walks) and then stretching exercises. Possibly more for a short-distance race, less for a longer distance.

Cool-down: Repeat of warm-up but without the strides.

The Race:

For a fitness runner—no races scheduled in this book, but try a low-key organized mile or 5K

For a mile to 10K runner, and a half-marathon to marathon runner—your target race on the final week of the program.

Race day—the event you've been working for.

© Human Kinetics

8

Progress Tracking

Knowing where you've been is as important as planning where you're going. This book makes it possible for you to preview and review on the same page. For each week's training in the various programs you have a page with the following information: the author's program for that week's training; your specific, personalized plans—times, distances, and paces—for that week; and your actual results for each day of that week. See the completed sample on page 79 and the blank page (page 80) for photocopying as needed.

Progress Reports

You're in luck. Whatever your goal is in running you have precise ways to measure your progress toward it.

Running is imminently measurable. You work with the objective standards of distance and time, not with subjective systems of points scored or comparisons with an opponent.

Say your goal is to increase the distance of your longest run or your total weekly distance. You know you've done it as soon as you add laps around the track or extend your road course. Or say your goal is to run a certain distance faster than ever before or to improve your overall pace. You know you've succeeded as soon as you look at your wrist-stopwatch and check the time.

Maybe your goals are even more personal. They might be centered less on how far and fast you run and more on how it makes you look and feel. You might run primarily to control your weight. You know if it's working each time you step on the bathroom scale.

You might run to keep your cardiovascular system in shape to boost your energy and endurance throughout the day. You can tell how effectively you're training this system by checking your resting pulse rate for the stronger, slower beats you're seeking.

Changes in performance results and physical signals do occur. They come to almost everyone who takes a serious approach to running at

© Brian Drake/SportsChrome USA

Tracking progress will help you look back and see how you've achieved your goals.

almost any age and initial state of fitness. But these changes don't come instantly—not overnight, not in a week, and not even in as long as a month. These are long-term reactions as the body slowly adapts to the work asked of it. A season from now, a year from now, a decade from now . . . then you can look back proudly at how far you've progressed. But where do you look? In the records you keep. We recommend that you keep a diary, journal, or log of your workouts. That way, you capture two of running's beauties: its measurability and comparability.

Distance, time, weight, and pulse are all quickly and easily measured. By writing them down today, you'll be able to compare them accurately with what you achieve in the near and distant future. Then you'll know exactly how far you have traveled. Your personal accounting can be as simple as a notation on a calendar or in a notebook. Or it can be as sophisticated as one of the published diaries or computer disks available commercially for this purpose. You might jot down a few quick numbers. Or you may add words of commentary about the experience. Where and how you keep your records doesn't matter. Just make sure to keep them consistently and to cover the essentials.

Performance Results

At the very least note the distance of each run and the time it took. Other factors you might include are the type of workout (easy, long, fast), the pace per mile or kilometer, the weather and terrain conditions, and how you felt.

Pay special attention to the harder workouts. These are the timed intervals, steady-state, and tempo runs, and races that give the best indications of your performance status. Compare them with previous workouts of the same type.

Physical Readings

Listen to your body. It's telling you how your training is going. Get in the habit of recording your resting pulse as you wake up each morning. A lowering of that reading over time means that your cardiovascular fitness is improving. If you notice a sudden jump of five beats or more in your heart rate it could mean that you're overtraining and need a rest. Know what your norm is so you can act when it changes.

Also, record your weight each morning. Most runners expect some long-term weight loss or at least to hold their weight at its present level. But a sudden drop of 3 pounds or more (1-plus kilograms) isn't a good sign. Again, it could signal that you've exceeded optimum training, and a break is best.

© Greg Crisp/SportsChrome USA

Running can give a sense of energy and enthusiasm—a feeling of satisfaction at having achieved a goal.

Remember This

Despite the ease of putting numbers to running results, the greatest value of running can't be measured in numbers. This value is the good feeling you develop from and for running. It's the feeling of energy and enthusiasm. It's the satisfaction of putting in solid efforts and the relaxation afterward. It's wanting to and being able to keep going and to keep coming back for more.

If running is to do all of this, you have to keep it up. It's an endurance activity, to be sure, but its benefits have a short life span. Stop for as little as a few weeks and they vanish, but keep running and they're constantly renewed, so your main goal is to continue. We want you to be out there running and profiting from it and enjoying it for a lifetime. This is winning in the truest sense. You win by lasting—and by outlasting those who get injured or lose interest and drop out. As the coaches like to say, "Winners never quit."

Sample Training Log

Here is a completed sample log page for someone preparing to run a 5K race. The runner's current best time at this distance is 20:27, for an estimated $\dot{V}O_2$max of 50. The goal, based on a $\dot{V}O_2$max of 54, is about 19:13—for a goal pace of 6:11 per mile (3:50 per kilometer). Maximum comfortable distance is 60 minutes.

5K Program: Week 12

Dates: May 26 to June 1

Weight: 144   Resting Pulse: 52

Week's Program

Day	Workout (priority)	Duration	Pace	%$\dot{V}O_2$max
Sunday	Long (1)	1/2 max+12 min	Moderate	60-70%
Monday	Recovery (5)	1/2 max time	Easy	50-60%
Tuesday	Race prep (3)	3 4 × 1 mile	Goal pace	See note
Wednesday	Recovery (6)	1/2 max time	Easy	50-60%
Thursday	Interval (2)	6 × 400 m	Strong	90-110%
Friday	Recovery (7)	1/2 max time	Easy	50-60%
Saturday	Recovery (4)	1/2 max time	Easy	50-60%

Week's Training

Day	Workout	Time	Distance	Pace
Sunday	long	42:05	5.0 miles 8.0 km	8:25/mile 5:12/km
Monday	recovery	29:55	2.9 miles 4.7 km	10:18/mile 6:23/km
Tuesday	interval	1:29 1:30 1:32 1:29 1:30 1:28	6 × 400 m	6:00/mile 3:43/km
Wednesday	recovery	30:00	3.0 miles 4.8 km	10:00/mile 6:12/km
Thursday	interval	1:29 1:30 1:32 1:29 1:30 1:28	6 × 400 m	6:00/mile 3:43/km
Friday	recovery	30:00	2.0 miles 3.2 km	15:00/mile 9:18/km
Saturday	recovery	30:10	3.1 miles 5.0 km	9:45/mile 6:02/km

Program: _____ Week #: _____

Dates: _____ to _____

Weight: _____ Resting pulse: _____

Week's Program

Day	Workout (priority)	Duration	Pace	%$\dot{V}O_2$max
Sunday				
Monday				
Tuesday				
Wednesday				
Thursday				
Friday				
Saturday				

Week's Training

Day	Workout	Time	Distance	Pace
Sunday				
Monday				
Tuesday				
Wednesday				
Thursday				
Friday				
Saturday				

(Photocopy this page for use as a training log.)

Scheduling Your Training

Here comes the exciting part. In part II you learned the individual ingredients of training. Now you mix them together, taking the workouts to the road, track, and trail and bringing those numbers to life.

The programs here are as personal as we can make them. They're based on your abilities and your goals. We started this customizing in chapter 6 by identifying those abilities and your goals for the next few months.

The programs in the next chapters are built on two cornerstones:

1. Your performance level as measured by running results from the recent past

2. Your choice of running emphasis in the months ahead

You aren't forever wedded to a performance level or to a single emphasis. We expect you to move among the many options as your fitness improves and your desire to explore this sport increases. However, your continued good health and accomplishment focus demand that you choose a training schedule that matches your current abilities and aims. We offer programs for six areas of emphasis:

- Beginning training (chapter 9): Use this program if you want to start running to improve your fitness level or resume after a lengthy pause.

- Fitness training (chapter 10): Use this program if you regularly run or run and walk primarily for exercise for relatively short distances and at relaxed paces.

- Recovery training (chapter 11): Use this program while you are recovering from an injury or a race.

- Short-race training (chapter 12): Use this program not only to prepare you for running a faster mile or 1500 meters but also for 5K up to 12K races.

- Half-marathon training (chapter 13): Use this program to make the big leap to a race more than twice the distance of a 10K and for 15K to 25K races.

- Marathon training (chapter 14): Use this program to train for the most prestigious event in distance running and for intermediate steps such as 30K and 20 miles.

Beginning Training

How do you start running if this is your first try at a formal program or if you're trying again after a lengthy pause? Begin by walking. "You must walk before you run" is a truism in this activity as well as the wider world.

Walk is not a bad four-letter word—or a sign of weakness or surrender. Walking is simply a point on a continuum stretching between strolling at one extreme and sprinting at the other. Walking benefits runners in many ways—as a warm-up or cool-down for runs, as a recovery break during interval training, as an alternative activity on rest days, as an exercise option during injury spells.

The safest way to launch a *running* program is to start *walking*. Can you walk easily and painlessly for a half-hour? If not, begin your fitness quest by working up to this level. Once you're walking the prerequisite 30 minutes, then you can run—in small amounts with walks in between. This is a form of interval training.

Measure the walk and run intervals by minutes, not by distance. This is simpler than measuring the route you take, and it removes the pressure of having to run a known distance at a known pace. Time yourself with a digital stopwatch, and put in a total of 30 minutes from the first day.

Runners should progress through the beginning programs at their own rates.

Run-walk three or four days a week, with at least one day off in between. On most of the *rest* days, simply walk the half-hour or substitute another cross-training activity, such as bicycling.

This chapter contains Joe Henderson's "Walk-to-Run Plan" that he uses when teaching beginning-running classes. Climb through the 10 steps listed, with walking decreasing as running periods increase.

All running in this program should feel comfortable to you, and a full *week's* training should feel easy before you advance. We list weekly training plans but urge you to progress at your own rate. Skip a week or more if the recommended sessions seem too easy for you, or repeat a week, or even drop back in the program as needed.

Once you can run 30 minutes steadily, you can graduate to the more advanced programs of later chapters. These programs have you run additional days per week, and you often run more than a half-hour (with or without walk breaks) and sometimes run less than 30 minutes, but at a faster pace. Follow the training for each of these 10 *weeks,* or steps, as recommended. After each day's training, record your results in the corresponding log.

Beginning Training: Week 1

Week's Program

Day	Total time	Run-walk mix	Total run
Sunday	30 min	Walk 25, run 5	25 min
Monday	Cross-train or rest		
Tuesday	30 min	Walk 25, run 5	5 min
Wednesday	Cross-train or rest		
Thursday	30 min	Walk 25, run 5	5 min
Friday	Cross-train or rest		
Saturday	30 min	Walk 25, run 5	5 min

Beginning Training: Week 2

Week's Program

Day	Total time	Run-walk mix	Total run
Sunday	Cross-train or rest		
Monday	30 min	Walk 10, run 5, walk 10, run 5	10 min
Tuesday	Cross-train or rest		
Wednesday	30 min	Walk 10, run 5, walk 10, run 5	10 min
Thursday	Cross-train or rest		
Friday	30 min	Walk 10, run 5, walk 10, run 5	10 min
Saturday	Cross-train or rest		

Week 1 Log

Dates: _____   to _____

Weight: _____   Resting pulse: _____

Week's Training

Day	Total time	Run-walk mix	Total run
Sunday			
Monday			
Tuesday			
Wednesday			
Thursday			
Friday			
Saturday			

Week 2 Log

Dates: _____   to _____

Weight: _____   Resting pulse: _____

Week's Training

Day	Total time	Run-walk mix	Total run
Sunday			
Monday			
Tuesday			
Wednesday			
Thursday			
Friday			
Saturday			

Beginning Training: Week 3

Week's Program

Day	Total time	Run-walk mix	Total run
Sunday	30 min	Walk 20, run 10	10 min
Monday	Cross-train or rest		
Tuesday	30 min	Walk 20, run 10	10 min
Wednesday	Cross-train or rest		
Thursday	30 min	Walk 20, run 10	10 min
Friday	Cross-train or rest		
Saturday	30 min	Walk 20, run 10	10 min

Beginning Training: Week 4

Week's Program

Day	Total time	Run-walk mix	Total run
Sunday	Cross-train or rest		
Monday	30 min	Walk 10, run 5, walk 5, run 10	15 min
Tuesday	Cross-train or rest		
Wednesday	30 min	Walk 10, run 5, walk 5, run 10	15 min
Thursday	Cross-train or rest		
Friday	30 min	Walk 10, run 5, walk 5, run 10	15 min
Saturday	Cross-train or rest		

Week 3 Log

Dates: _____   to _____

Weight: _____   Resting pulse: _____

Week's Training

Day	Total time	Run-walk mix	Total run
Sunday			
Monday			
Tuesday			
Wednesday			
Thursday			
Friday			
Saturday			

Week 4 Log

Dates: _____   to _____

Weight: _____   Resting pulse: _____

Week's Training

Day	Total time	Run-walk mix	Total run
Sunday			
Monday			
Tuesday			
Wednesday			
Thursday			
Friday			
Saturday			

Beginning Training: Week 5

Week's Program

Day	Total time	Run-walk mix	Total run
Sunday	30 min	Walk 15, run 15	15 min
Monday	Cross-train or rest		
Tuesday	30 min	Walk 15, run 15	15 min
Wednesday	Cross-train or rest		
Thursday	30 min	Walk 15, run 15	15 min
Friday	Cross-train or rest		
Saturday	30 min	Walk 15, run 15	15 min

Beginning Training: Week 6

Week's Program

Day	Total time	Run-walk mix	Total run
Sunday	Cross-train or rest		
Monday	30 min	Walk 5, run 5, walk 5, run 15	20 min
Tuesday	Cross-train or rest		
Wednesday	30 min	Walk 5, run 5, walk 5, run 15	20 min
Thursday	Cross-train or rest		
Friday	30 min	Walk 5, run 5, walk 5, run 15	20 min
Saturday	Cross-train or rest		

Week 5 Log

Dates: _____ to _____

Weight: _____ Resting pulse: _____

Week's Training

Day	Total time	Run-walk mix	Total run
Sunday			
Monday			
Tuesday			
Wednesday			
Thursday			
Friday			
Saturday			

Week 6 Log

Dates: _____ to _____

Weight: _____ Resting pulse: _____

Week's Training

Day	Total time	Run-walk mix	Total run
Sunday			
Monday			
Tuesday			
Wednesday			
Thursday			
Friday			
Saturday			

Beginning Training: Week 7

Week's Program

Day	Total time	Run-walk mix	Total run
Sunday	30 min	Walk 10, run 20	20 min
Monday	Cross-train or rest		
Tuesday	30 min	Walk 10, run 20	20 min
Wednesday	Cross-train or rest		
Thursday	30 min	Walk 10, run 20	20 min
Friday	Cross-train or rest		
Saturday	30 min	Walk 10, run 20	20 min

Beginning Training: Week 8

Week's Program

Day	Total time	Run-walk mix	Total run
Sunday	Cross-train or rest		
Monday	30 min	Run 5, walk 5, run 20	25 min
Tuesday	Cross-train or rest		
Wednesday	30 min	Run 5, walk 5, run 20	25 min
Thursday	Cross-train or rest		
Friday	30 min	Run 5, walk 5, run 20	25 min
Saturday	Cross-train or rest		

Week 7 Log

Dates: _____   to _____

Weight: _____   Resting pulse: _____

Week's Training

Day	Total time	Run-walk mix	Total run
Sunday			
Monday			
Tuesday			
Wednesday			
Thursday			
Friday			
Saturday			

Week 8 Log

Dates: _____   to _____

Weight: _____   Resting pulse: _____

Week's Training

Day	Total time	Run-walk mix	Total run
Sunday			
Monday			
Tuesday			
Wednesday			
Thursday			
Friday			
Saturday			

Beginning Training: Week 9

Week's Program

Day	Total time	Run-walk mix	Total run
Sunday	30 min	Walk 5, run 25	25 min
Monday	Cross-train or rest		
Tuesday	30 min	Walk 5, run 25	25 min
Wednesday	Cross-train or rest		
Thursday	30 min	Walk 5, run 25	25 min
Friday	Cross-train or rest		
Saturday	30 min	Walk 5, run 25	25 min

Beginning Training: Week 10

Week's Program

Day	Total time	Run-walk mix	Total run
Sunday	Cross-train or rest		
Monday	30 min	Run all 30	30 min
Tuesday	Cross-train or rest		
Wednesday	30 min	Run all 30	30 min
Thursday	Cross-train or rest		
Friday	30 min	Run all 30	30 min
Saturday	Cross-train or rest		

Week 9 Log

Dates: _____   to _____

Weight: _____   Resting pulse: _____

Week's Training

Day	Total time	Run-walk mix	Total run
Sunday			
Monday			
Tuesday			
Wednesday			
Thursday			
Friday			
Saturday			

Week 10 Log

Dates: _____   to _____

Weight: _____   Resting pulse: _____

Week's Training

Day	Total time	Run-walk mix	Total run
Sunday			
Monday			
Tuesday			
Wednesday			
Thursday			
Friday			
Saturday			

Fitness Training

Fitness running also goes by the name *jogging,* a term that some runners find distasteful and that we won't use again. Running purely for fitness, as opposed to training for races, is a perfectly honorable pursuit.

You run for the aerobic benefits, weight control, stress management, and similar personal-fitness reasons. And you run enough to test yourself in organized fun-runs up to 5K (3.1 miles) in length, if you're so tempted.

The program outlined here lasts 13 weeks, or three months, or one season of the year. Train three to four days each week. The priority numbers indicate a workout's order of importance with one being the most important and seven being the least. When you run fewer days than seven, drop workouts from the highest number (7) downward. Determine appropriate lengths and paces of your runs from the tables in chapter 6. Remember from chapter 7 that SWS stands for somewhat strong. Then take this information and plug these figures into the training formulas supplied on the weekly log pages.

Note that some formulas offer a range of choices for duration of a run or number of repetitions. Base your selections on your current fitness level.

For tempo workouts (starting in week 4) add a warm-up of a five- to six-minute jog and 4 × 50-meter strides with slower ones of equal length. For example, 400 meters total with recovery jog/walks of 50 meters in between each. Also add a cool-down jog of three to five minutes.

After finishing the workout, record your results in the weekly log provided here.

Fitness Training: Week 1

Week's Program

Day	Workout (priority)	Duration	Pace	%$\dot{V}O_2$max
Sunday	Long (1)	Max time	Moderate	60-70%
Monday	Recovery (5)	1/2 max time	Easy	50-60%
Tuesday	Recovery (4)	1/2 max time	Easy	50-60%
Wednesday	Steady state (2)	2/3 max time	SWS	75-85%
Thursday	Recovery (7)	1/2 max time	Easy	50-60%
Friday	Steady state (3)	2/3 max time	SWS	75-85%
Saturday	Recovery (6)	1/2 max time	Easy	50-60%

Fitness Training: Week 2

Week's Program

Day	Workout (priority)	Duration	Pace	%$\dot{V}O_2$max
Sunday	Long (1)	Max+1 min	Moderate	60-70%
Monday	Recovery (5)	1/2 max time	Easy	50-60%
Tuesday	Recovery (4)	1/2 max time	Easy	50-60%
Wednesday	Steady state (2)	2/3 max+1 min	SWS	75-85%
Thursday	Recovery (7)	1/2 max time	Easy	50-60%
Friday	Steady state (3)	2/3 max time	SWS	75-85%
Saturday	Recovery (6)	1/2 max time	Easy	50-60%

Week 1 Log

Dates: _____ to _____

Weight: _____ Resting pulse: _____

Week's Training

Day	Workout	Time	Distance	Pace
Sunday				
Monday				
Tuesday				
Wednesday				
Thursday				
Friday				
Saturday				

Week 2 Log

Dates: _____ to _____

Weight: _____ Resting pulse: _____

Week's Training

Day	Workout	Time	Distance	Pace
Sunday				
Monday				
Tuesday				
Wednesday				
Thursday				
Friday				
Saturday				

Fitness Training

Fitness Training: Week 3

Week's Program

Day	Workout (priority)	Duration	Pace	%$\dot{V}O_2$max
Sunday	Long (1)	Max+2 min	Moderate	60-70%
Monday	Recovery (5)	1/2 max time	Easy	50-60%
Tuesday	Recovery (4)	1/2 max time	Easy	50-60%
Wednesday	Steady state (2)	2/3 max+2 min	SWS	75-85%
Thursday	Recovery (7)	1/2 max time	Easy	50-60%
Friday	Steady state (3)	2/3 max time	SWS	75-85%
Saturday	Recovery (6)	1/4-1/2 max	Easy	50-60%

Fitness Training: Week 4

Week's Program

Day	Workout (priority)	Duration	Pace	%$\dot{V}O_2$max
Sunday	Tempo (1)	1/2 max time	SWS to strong	85%
Monday	Recovery (5)	1/2 max time	Easy	50-60%
Tuesday	Recovery (3)	1/2 max time	Easy	50-60%
Wednesday	Recovery (7)	1/2 max time	Easy	50-60%
Thursday	Steady state (2)	2/3 max+3 min	SWS	75-85%
Friday	Recovery (6)	1/2 max time	Easy	50-60%
Saturday	Recovery (4)	1/2 max time	Easy	50-60%

Week 3 Log

Dates: _____ to _____

Weight: _____ Resting pulse: _____

Week's Training

Day	Workout	Time	Distance	Pace
Sunday				
Monday				
Tuesday				
Wednesday				
Thursday				
Friday				
Saturday				

Week 4 Log

Dates: _____ to _____

Weight: _____ Resting pulse: _____

Week's Training

Day	Workout	Time	Distance	Pace
Sunday				
Monday				
Tuesday				
Wednesday				
Thursday				
Friday				
Saturday				

Fitness Training: Week 5

Week's Program

Day	Workout (priority)	Duration	Pace	%$\dot{V}O_2$max
Sunday	Long (1)	Max+3 min	Moderate	60-70%
Monday	Recovery (5)	1/2 max time	Easy	50-60%
Tuesday	Recovery (4)	1/2 max time	Easy	50-60%
Wednesday	Steady state (2)	2/3 max+4 min	SWS	75-85%
Thursday	Recovery (7)	1/2 max time	Easy	50-60%
Friday	Steady state (3)	2/3 max time	SWS	75-85%
Saturday	Recovery (6)	1/2 max time	Easy	50-60%

Fitness Training: Week 6

Week's Program

Day	Workout (priority)	Duration	Pace	%$\dot{V}O_2$max
Sunday	Long (1)	Max+4 min	Moderate	60-70%
Monday	Recovery (5)	1/2 max time	Easy	50-60%
Tuesday	Recovery (4)	1/2 max time	Easy	50-60%
Wednesday	Steady state (2)	2/3 max+5 min	SWS	75-85%
Thursday	Recovery (7)	1/2 max time	Easy	50-60%
Friday	Steady state (3)	2/3 max time	SWS	75-85%
Saturday	Recovery (6)	1/2 max time	Easy	50-60%

Week 5 Log

Dates: _____   to _____

Weight: _____   Resting pulse: _____

Week's Training

Day	Workout	Time	Distance	Pace
Sunday				
Monday				
Tuesday				
Wednesday				
Thursday				
Friday				
Saturday				

Week 6 Log

Dates: _____   to _____

Weight: _____   Resting pulse: _____

Week's Training

Day	Workout	Time	Distance	Pace
Sunday				
Monday				
Tuesday				
Wednesday				
Thursday				
Friday				
Saturday				

Fitness Training: Week 7

Week's Program

Day	Workout (priority)	Duration	Pace	%$\dot{V}O_2$max
Sunday	Long (1)	Max+5 min	Moderate	60-70%
Monday	Recovery (5)	1/2 max time	Easy	50-60%
Tuesday	Recovery (4)	1/2 max time	Easy	50-60%
Wednesday	Steady state (2)	2/3 max+6 min	SWS	75-85%
Thursday	Recovery (7)	1/2 max time	Easy	50-60%
Friday	Steady state (3)	2/3 max time	SWS	75-85%
Saturday	Recovery (6)	1/4-1/2 max	Easy	50-60%

Fitness Training: Week 8

Week's Program

Day	Workout (priority)	Duration	Pace	%$\dot{V}O_2$max
Sunday	Tempo (1)	1/2 max time	SWS to strong	85%
Monday	Recovery (5)	1/2 max time	Easy	50-60%
Tuesday	Recovery (3)	1/2 max time	Easy	50-60%
Wednesday	Recovery (7)	1/2 max time	Easy	50-60%
Thursday	Steady state (2)	2/3 max+6 min	SWS	75-85%
Friday	Recovery (6)	1/2 max time	Easy	50-60%
Saturday	Recovery (4)	1/4-1/2 max	Easy	50-60%

Week 7 Log

Dates: _____   to _____

Weight: _____   Resting pulse: _____

Week's Training

Day	Workout	Time	Distance	Pace
Sunday				
Monday				
Tuesday				
Wednesday				
Thursday				
Friday				
Saturday				

Week 8 Log

Dates: _____   to _____

Weight: _____   Resting pulse: _____

Week's Training

Day	Workout	Time	Distance	Pace
Sunday				
Monday				
Tuesday				
Wednesday				
Thursday				
Friday				
Saturday				

Fitness Training: Week 9

Week's Program

Day	Workout (priority)	Duration	Pace	%$\dot{V}O_2$max
Sunday	Long (1)	Max+6 min	Moderate	60-70%
Monday	Recovery (5)	1/2 max time	Easy	50-60%
Tuesday	Recovery (4)	1/2 max time	Easy	50-60%
Wednesday	Steady state (2)	2/3 max+6 min	SWS	75-85%
Thursday	Recovery (7)	1/2 max time	Easy	50-60%
Friday	Steady state (3)	2/3 max time	SWS	75-85%
Saturday	Recovery (6)	1/2 max time	Easy	50-60%

Fitness Training: Week 10

Week's Program

Day	Workout (priority)	Duration	Pace	%$\dot{V}O_2$max
Sunday	Long (1)	Max+7 min	Moderate	60-70%
Monday	Recovery (5)	1/2 max time	Easy	50-60%
Tuesday	Recovery (4)	1/2 max time	Easy	50-60%
Wednesday	Steady state (2)	2/3 max+6 min	SWS	75-85%
Thursday	Recovery (7)	1/2 max time	Easy	50-60%
Friday	Steady state (3)	2/3 max time	SWS	75-85%
Saturday	Recovery (6)	1/2 max time	Easy	50-60%

Week 9 Log

Dates: _____   to _____

Weight: _____   Resting pulse: _____

Week's Training

Day	Workout	Time	Distance	Pace
Sunday				
Monday				
Tuesday				
Wednesday				
Thursday				
Friday				
Saturday				

Week 10 Log

Dates: _____   to _____

Weight: _____   Resting pulse: _____

Week's Training

Day	Workout	Time	Distance	Pace
Sunday				
Monday				
Tuesday				
Wednesday				
Thursday				
Friday				
Saturday				

Fitness Training: Week 11

Week's Program

Day	Workout (priority)	Duration	Pace	%$\dot{V}O_2$max
Sunday	Long (1)	Max+8 min	Moderate	60-70%
Monday	Recovery (5)	1/2 max time	Easy	50-60%
Tuesday	Recovery (4)	1/2 max time	Easy	50-60%
Wednesday	Steady state (2)	2/3 max+6 min	SWS	75-85%
Thursday	Recovery (7)	1/2 max time	Easy	50-60%
Friday	Steady state (3)	2/3 max time	SWS	75-85%
Saturday	Recovery (6)	1/2 max time	Easy	50-60%

Fitness Training: Week 12

Week's Program

Day	Workout (priority)	Duration	Pace	%$\dot{V}O_2$max
Sunday	Tempo (1)	1/2 max time	SWS to strong	85%
Monday	Recovery (5)	1/2 max time	Easy	50-60%
Tuesday	Recovery (3)	1/2 max time	Easy	50-60%
Wednesday	Recovery (7)	1/2 max time	Easy	50-60%
Thursday	Steady state (2)	2/3 max+6 min	SWS	75-85%
Friday	Recovery (6)	1/2 max time	Easy	50-60%
Saturday	Recovery (4)	1/2 max time	Easy	50-60%

Week 11 Log

Dates: _____ to _____

Weight: _____ Resting pulse: _____

Week's Training

Day	Workout	Time	Distance	Pace
Sunday				
Monday				
Tuesday				
Wednesday				
Thursday				
Friday				
Saturday				

Week 12 Log

Dates: _____ to _____

Weight: _____ Resting pulse: _____

Week's Training

Day	Workout	Time	Distance	Pace
Sunday				
Monday				
Tuesday				
Wednesday				
Thursday				
Friday				
Saturday				

Fitness Training: Week 13

Week's Program

Day	Workout (priority)	Duration	Pace	%$\dot{V}O_2$max
Sunday	Steady state (2)	2/3 max+7 min	SWS	75-85%
Monday	Recovery (4)	1/4 max time	Easy	50-60%
Tuesday	Recovery (7)	1/4 max time	Easy	50-60%
Wednesday	Steady state (3)	2/3 max+7 min	SWS	75-85%
Thursday	Recovery (5)	1/4 max time	Easy	50-60%
Friday	Recovery (6)	1/4 max time	Easy	50-60%
Saturday	Long (1)	Max+10 min	Moderate	60-70%

Week 13 Log

Dates: _____   to _____

Weight: _____   Resting pulse: _____

Week's Training

Day	Workout	Time	Distance	Pace
Sunday				
Monday				
Tuesday				
Wednesday				
Thursday				
Friday				
Saturday				

11

Recovery Training

Progress in a running program doesn't proceed along a steady upward slope. As you climb toward peaks, you're almost certain to dip into valleys along the way.

These low spots are unplanned setbacks—usually caused by injury or illness but also a result of personal or work conflicts that disrupt training plans. You also encounter voluntary valleys, in the form of necessary downtime after big races or hard seasons of racing.

This chapter tells how to climb out of these valleys. The two most common running lulls are for recovery from an injury or a major race. We're assuming that your rehab begins right after the injury or exhausting competition and that you've retained your fitness. However, if you had to stop running for a month or more, reread chapter 9 for advice on beginning again.

Recovering From Injuries

Most running injuries are self-caused. That is, they aren't accidents (such as falling into a hole or tripping over a dog) but brought on by running itself. You run farther, faster, or more frequently than your body can handle, and it rebels by breaking down. That's the bad news. The good: Few of these injuries are serious if you catch them early, and you can recover from them rather quickly just by modifying your activity. We can't give you an exact rehab program, because the degree of damage and speed of recovery vary widely from runner to runner. We can give guidelines for progressing by stages back to normal running training.

Listen closely to your body's signals, and accept pain as a friend who's telling you what you should and shouldn't do. If you try to rush progress you may end up slipping backward through the stages. This list of stages of an injury comes from Joe Henderson's book, *Running 101*. If you're coming back from an illness, substitute the word *fatigue* for *pain*, and work up from stage 2.

- Stage 1: Walking is painful, but running is impossible. Bike or swim during your usual running time. These activities don't put pressure on most injuries, but they still provide steady training. They let you feel that you retain some control over your physical life.
- Stage 2: Walking is relatively pain-free, but running still hurts. Start to walk—for the same amount of time as your normal runs—as soon as you can move ahead without limping. Continue as long as the pain is tolerable. (These limitations apply at all stages of recovery.)
- Stage 3: Walking is easy, and some running is possible. As walking becomes too easy, add intervals of slow running—as little as one minute in five at first, then gradually build up the amount of running until you reach the next level.
- Stage 4: Running pain eases, but minor discomfort persists. The balance tips in favor of running mixed with walking. Insert brief periods of walking at this level when pain returns during the steady pounding from running.
- Stage 5: All pain and tenderness blessedly is gone. Run again, but approach each outing cautiously for a while as you regain lost fitness. Run a little slower than normal, with no long or fast efforts—and few hills and definitely no races—until you can handle the short, slow runs comfortably.

Only after you've passed stage 5 are you ready to resume normal training and racing. The injury has been worthwhile if it taught you what got you into this trouble and if you learned not to make the mistake again.

Recovering From Races

Racing is hard work. It's challenging, motivating, and exciting, to be sure. But as you push yourself harder in the race-day crowd than you ever could alone, the race takes a toll that must be repaid. The longer the race, the greater the toll and the time needed to repay it. For instance, you might feel fine to run a few days after a 5K—but you might be too sore a few days after a marathon.

As with injuries, we can't give exact programs for postrace recovery because it varies so widely for race distances. We can tell you that runners recover at fairly predictable rates as they pass through three stages of recovery. In his book *Running 101*, Henderson quotes the commonly used Foster Formula (named for New Zealand marathon great Jack Foster). It calls for one day of easy running or rest for each mile of the race. For example, if your race was a 10K (6.2 miles), you need about a week to recover. If you ran a marathon (26.2 miles or 42.2K), you'll need nearly a month for your body to heal. This doesn't mean you don't run during this recovery period, but you should avoid long or fast training and any new race.

Henderson says that one easy day per *kilometer* might serve as an even better guideline, especially for older runners whose recovery rate typically has slowed with age. Using this formula, the R & R (recovery and rebuilding) period works out to 1-1/2 weeks after a 10K and 6 weeks after a marathon.

Whether it's one day per mile or a day per K, the recovery timetable accounts for the normal stages of rebuilding after an all-out racing effort. Each stage demands more recovery time than the one before.

• Stage 1: Soreness. Certain muscles hurt the next day, and they often hurt worse the day after that because of a phenomenon known as delayed-onset muscle soreness, or DOMS. Wait out this condition, which usually passes soon after it has peaked 48 to 72 hours after the race. Run little if any, because overworking stressed legs only invites injury. If you're itching for more activity, make it something other than running—such as walking, bicycling, or swimming.

• Stage 2: Tiredness. Nothing specifically hurts anymore, but you feel vaguely sluggish and low on energy. You might, after a long race, want to eat and drink and sleep more than normal. These are signs that the body is still healing. Indulge it by taking nothing but easy runs, perhaps supplementing them with cross-training.

• Stage 3: Laziness. Your body feels fine, but your head still isn't in the game. Your training runs aren't exciting, and you're unmotivated to try another race. Marathoners call this condition the *postmarathon blues*. This is normal and even necessary—it's the mind's way of protecting the body, forcing you to take the full quota of recovery time. You'll be ready to run another race when you forget how hard the last one felt, and then you'll regain your excitement for long and fast training.

We provide six weeks of log pages here. This is long enough for most injuries to heal and for your body to recover from races as long as a marathon. In the weekly logs, record each day's training plans and results until you're ready to return to your normal program of choice in a later chapter.

Week 1 Log

Dates: _____   to _____

Weight: _____   Resting pulse: _____

Week's Training

Day	Day's plans	Day's results
Sunday		
Monday		
Tuesday		
Wednesday		
Thursday		
Friday		
Saturday		

Week 2 Log

Dates: _____   to _____

Weight: _____   Resting pulse: _____

Week's Training

Day	Day's plans	Day's results
Sunday		
Monday		
Tuesday		
Wednesday		
Thursday		
Friday		
Saturday		

Week 3 Log

Dates: _____ to _____

Weight: _____ Resting pulse: _____

Week's Training

Day	Day's plans	Day's results
Sunday		
Monday		
Tuesday		
Wednesday		
Thursday		
Friday		
Saturday		

Week 4 Log

Dates: _____ to _____

Weight: _____ Resting pulse: _____

Week's Training

Day	Day's plans	Day's results
Sunday		
Monday		
Tuesday		
Wednesday		
Thursday		
Friday		
Saturday		

Week 5 Log

Dates: _____   to _____

Weight: _____   Resting pulse: _____

Week's Training

Day	Day's plans	Day's results
Sunday		
Monday		
Tuesday		
Wednesday		
Thursday		
Friday		
Saturday		

Week 6 Log

Dates: _____   to _____

Weight: _____   Resting pulse: _____

Week's Training

Day	Day's plans	Day's results
Sunday		
Monday		
Tuesday		
Wednesday		
Thursday		
Friday		
Saturday		

Short-Race Training

The word *short* is a relative term. To someone whose daily run ends at a half-hour or less, a race of 30 to 60 minutes doesn't sound *short*. Or when you run all-out for even 1 mile or 1-1/2 kilometers, the distance doesn't feel *short*.

The distances we cover in this chapter are short in comparison with other road races. They're the shortest events that a distance runner will race—1500 meters or 1 mile on the track, and 5K to 10K on the track, road, or cross-country. The 5K and 10K runs are the most common road-race distances.

When someone who doesn't run hears you are a runner, the first question will likely be, "How fast do you run a mile?" This is true even in many countries that use the metric system to measure distance. The mile and its metric versions, 1500 and 1600 meters, are track's most popular races.

The 5K, or five-kilometer distance, carries different meanings to different groups of runners. On the track it goes by the name 5000 meters. The 5K is a common cross-country distance in high school. Mostly it's a road distance and the race length that draws the greatest number of runners. Even here you find variety: The 5K serves as an entry point for new racers and also as a place where experienced runners race their fastest.

When mass-participation road racing first grew up in the 1970s, the 10K spurred much of that growth. It was the street version of the track 10,000 meters. This is the distance of such classic races as Peachtree in Atlanta and Bolder Boulder in Colorado, both of which draw about 50,000 participants. The slightly longer 12K, such as Bay to Breakers in San Francisco and Bloomsday in Spokane, Washington, attract even more runners.

Training is quite similar for the whole range of short distances— 1500 meters or mile to 10K or 12K—so we combine them into a single program. Its best results, however, come at or near the 5K distance. Train three to six days each week if you're a casual racer, four to seven days if advanced. Priority numbers indicate a workout's order of importance, with priority one being the most important, seven the least. When you run fewer days than seven, drop workouts from the highest number (7) downward. Determine appropriate lengths and paces of your runs from the tables in chapter 6. Remember from chapter 7 that SWS stands for somewhat strong. Then take this information and plug these figures into the training formulas supplied on the weekly log pages. Note that some formulas offer a range of choices for duration of a run or number of repetitions. Base your selections on your current fitness level.

For tempo, interval, speed, and race-preparation workouts, add a warm-up of a 5- to 10-minute jog and 4×50-meter strides with slower ones of equal length (for example, 400 meters total with recovery jog/walks of 50 meters in between each). Also add a cool-down jog of 5 to 10 minutes.

For all repetition-type workouts (strides, interval, speed, race-preparation), follow the faster segment with a slower one of equal length (for example, 4×400 meters with a 400-meter recovery jog/walk in between each).

When you train for goal-pace runs, select a pace that corresponds to your $\dot{V}O_2$max plus four points. For example, a runner with a current reading of 50 has a goal-pace $\dot{V}O_2$max of 54.

After finishing the workout, record your results in the weekly log provided here.

Similar programs can be used to train for 5K up to 12K distances.

© Paul McMahon

Short-Race Training: Week 1

Week's Program

Day	Workout (priority)	Duration	Pace	%$\dot{V}O_2$max
Sunday	Long (1)	Max time	Moderate	60-70%
Monday	Recovery (5)	1/2 max time	Easy	50-60%
Tuesday	Speed (4)	5 × 100 m	Strong	90-110%
Wednesday	Steady state (2)	2/3 max time	SWS	75-85%
Thursday	Recovery (7)	1/2 max time	Easy	50-60%
Friday	Steady state (3)	2/3 max time	SWS	75-85%
Saturday	Recovery (6)	1/2 max time	Easy	50-60%

Short-Race Training: Week 2

Week's Program

Day	Workout (priority)	Duration	Pace	%$\dot{V}O_2$max
Sunday	Long (1)	Max+2-4 min	Moderate	60-70%
Monday	Recovery (5)	1/2 max time	Easy	50-60%
Tuesday	Speed (4)	7-8 × 100 m	Strong	90-110%
Wednesday	Steady state (2)	2/3 max+1-2 min	SWS	75-85%
Thursday	Recovery (7)	1/2 max time	Easy	50-60%
Friday	Steady state (3)	2/3 max time	SWS	75-85%
Saturday	Recovery (6)	1/2 max time	Easy	50-60%

Week 1 Log

Dates: _____ to _____

Weight: _____ Resting pulse: _____

Week's Training

Day	Workout	Time	Distance	Pace
Sunday				
Monday				
Tuesday				
Wednesday				
Thursday				
Friday				
Saturday				

Week 2 Log

Dates: _____ to _____

Weight: _____ Resting pulse: _____

Week's Training

Day	Workout	Time	Distance	Pace
Sunday				
Monday				
Tuesday				
Wednesday				
Thursday				
Friday				
Saturday				

Short-Race Training: Week 3

Week's Program

Day	Workout (priority)	Duration	Pace	%$\dot{V}O_2$max
Sunday	Long (1)	Max+4-6 min	Moderate	60-70%
Monday	Recovery (5)	1/2 max time	Easy	50-60%
Tuesday	Speed (4)	4-6 × 200 m	Strong	90-110%
Wednesday	Steady state (2)	2/3 max+2-3 min	SWS	75-85%
Thursday	Recovery (7)	1/2 max time	Easy	50-60%
Friday	Steady state (3)	2/3 max time	SWS	75-85%
Saturday	Recovery (6)	1/4-1/2 max	Easy	50-60%

Short-Race Training: Week 4

Week's Program

Day	Workout (priority)	Duration	Pace	%$\dot{V}O_2$max
Sunday	Tempo (1)	1/2 max time	SWS to strong	85%
Monday	Recovery (5)	1/2 max time	Easy	50-60%
Tuesday	Interval (3)	3-5 × 300 m	Strong	90-110%
Wednesday	Recovery (7)	1/2 max time	Easy	50-60%
Thursday	Steady state (2)	2/3 max+2-4 min	SWS	75-85%
Friday	Recovery (6)	1/2 max time	Easy	50-60%
Saturday	Speed (4)	7-10 × 100 m	Strong	90-110%

Week 3 Log

Dates: _____ to _____

Weight: _____ Resting pulse: _____

Week's Training

Day	Workout	Time	Distance	Pace
Sunday				
Monday				
Tuesday				
Wednesday				
Thursday				
Friday				
Saturday				

Week 4 Log

Dates: _____ to _____

Weight: _____ Resting pulse: _____

Week's Training

Day	Workout	Time	Distance	Pace
Sunday				
Monday				
Tuesday				
Wednesday				
Thursday				
Friday				
Saturday				

Short-Race Training: Week 5

Week's Program

Day	Workout (priority)	Duration	Pace	%$\dot{V}O_2$max
Sunday	Long (1)	Max+6-8 min	moderate	60-70%
Monday	Recovery (5)	1/2 max time	easy	50-60%
Tuesday	Speed (4)	8-10 × 100 m	strong	90-110%
Wednesday	Steady state (2)	2/3 max+3-5 min	SWS	75-85%
Thursday	Recovery (7)	1/2 max time	easy	50-60%
Friday	Steady state (3)	2/3 max time	SWS	75-85%
Saturday	Recovery (6)	1/2 max time	easy	50-60%

Short-Race Training: Week 6

Week's Program

Day	Workout (priority)	Duration	Pace	%$\dot{V}O_2$max
Sunday	Long (1)	Max+8-10 min	Moderate	60-70%
Monday	Recovery (5)	1/2 max time	Easy	50-60%
Tuesday	Speed (4)	10 × 100 m	Strong	90-110%
Wednesday	Steady state (2)	2/3 max+4-6 min	SWS	75-85%
Thursday	Recovery (7)	1/2 max time	Easy	50-60%
Friday	Steady state (3)	2/3 max time	SWS	75-85%
Saturday	Recovery (6)	1/2 max time	Easy	50-60%

Week 5 Log

Dates: _____   to _____

Weight: _____   Resting pulse: _____

Week's Training

Day	Workout	Time	Distance	Pace
Sunday				
Monday				
Tuesday				
Wednesday				
Thursday				
Friday				
Saturday				

Week 6 Log

Dates: _____   to _____

Weight: _____   Resting pulse: _____

Week's Training

Day	Workout	Time	Distance	Pace
Sunday				
Monday				
Tuesday				
Wednesday				
Thursday				
Friday				
Saturday				

Short-Race Training: Week 7

Week's Program

Day	Workout (priority)	Duration	Pace	%$\dot{V}O_2$max
Sunday	Long (1)	Max+10-12 min	Moderate	60-70%
Monday	Recovery (5)	1/2 max time	Easy	50-60%
Tuesday	Interval (4)	6-10 × 200 m	Strong	90-110%
Wednesday	Steady state (2)	2/3 max+4-6 min	SWS	75-85%
Thursday	Recovery (7)	1/2 max time	Easy	50-60%
Friday	Steady state (3)	2/3 max time	SWS	75-85%
Saturday	Recovery (6)	1/4-1/2 max	Easy	50-60%

Short-Race Training: Week 8

Week's Program

Day	Workout (priority)	Duration	Pace	%$\dot{V}O_2$max
Sunday	Tempo (1)	1/2 max time	SWS to strong	85%
Monday	Recovery (5)	1/2 max time	Easy	50-60%
Tuesday	Interval (3)	5-7 × 300 m	Strong	90-110%
Wednesday	Recovery (7)	1/2 max time	Easy	50-60%
Thursday	Steady state (2)	2/3 max+4-6 min	SWS	75-85%
Friday	Recovery (6)	1/2 max time	Easy	50-60%
Saturday	Speed (4)	10 × 100 m	Strong	90-110%

Week 7 Log

Dates: _____ to _____

Weight: _____ Resting pulse: _____

Week's Training

Day	Workout	Time	Distance	Pace
Sunday				
Monday				
Tuesday				
Wednesday				
Thursday				
Friday				
Saturday				

Week 8 Log

Dates: _____ to _____

Weight: _____ Resting pulse: _____

Week's Training

Day	Workout	Time	Distance	Pace
Sunday				
Monday				
Tuesday				
Wednesday				
Thursday				
Friday				
Saturday				

Short-Race Training: Week 9

Week's Program

Day	Workout (priority)	Duration	Pace	%$\dot{V}O_2$max
Sunday	Long (1)	Max+11-14 min	Moderate	60-70%
Monday	Recovery (5)	1/2 max time	Easy	50-60%
Tuesday	Interval (2)	4-6 × 400 m	Strong	90-110%
Wednesday	Recovery (7)	1/2 max time	Easy	50-60%
Thursday	Interval (3)	8-10 × 200 m	Strong	90-110%
Friday	Recovery (6)	1/2 max time	Easy	50-60%
Saturday	Speed (4)	10-12 × 100 m	Strong	90-110%

Short-Race Training: Week 10

Week's Program

Day	Workout (priority)	Duration	Pace	%$\dot{V}O_2$max
Sunday	Tempo (1)	1/2 max time	SWS to strong	85%-95%
Monday	Recovery (5)	1/2 max time	Easy	50-60%
Tuesday	Interval (3)	5-8 × 400 m	Strong	90-110%
Wednesday	Recovery (7)	1/2 max time	Easy	50-60%
Thursday	Steady state (2)	2/3 max+5-7 min	SWS	75-85%
Friday	Recovery (6)	1/2 max time	Easy	50-60%
Saturday	Speed (4)	10-12 × 100 m	Strong	90-110%

Week 9 Log

Dates: _____   to _____

Weight: _____   Resting pulse: _____

Week's Training

Day	Workout	Time	Distance	Pace
Sunday				
Monday				
Tuesday				
Wednesday				
Thursday				
Friday				
Saturday				

Week 10 Log

Dates: _____   to _____

Weight: _____   Resting pulse: _____

Week's Training

Day	Workout	Time	Distance	Pace
Sunday				
Monday				
Tuesday				
Wednesday				
Thursday				
Friday				
Saturday				

Short-Race Training: Week 11

Week's Program

Day	Workout (priority)	Duration	Pace	%$\dot{V}O_2$max
Sunday	Race prep (2)	3 × 1 mile	Goal pace	See intro
Monday	Recovery (5)	1/2 max time	Easy	50-60%
Tuesday	Race prep (3)	6 × 800 m	Goal pace	See intro
Wednesday	Recovery (6)	1/2 max time	Easy	50-60%
Thursday	Interval (1)	5-8 × 200 m	Strong	90-110%
Friday	Recovery (7)	1/2 max time	Easy	50-60%
Saturday	Recovery (4)	1/2 max time	Easy	50-60%

Short-Race Training: Week 12

Week's Program

Day	Workout (priority)	Duration	Pace	%$\dot{V}O_2$max
Sunday	Long (1)	1/2 max+12 min	Moderate	60-70%
Monday	Recovery (5)	1/2 max time	Easy	50-60%
Tuesday	Race prep (3)	3-4 × 1 mile	Goal pace	See intro
Wednesday	Recovery (6)	1/2 max time	Easy	50-60%
Thursday	Interval (2)	6 × 400 m	Strong	90-110%
Friday	Recovery (7)	1/2 max time	Easy	50-60%
Saturday	Recovery (4)	1/2 max time	Easy	50-60%

Week 11 Log

Dates: _____   to _____

Weight: _____   Resting pulse: _____

Week's Training

Day	Workout	Time	Distance	Pace
Sunday				
Monday				
Tuesday				
Wednesday				
Thursday				
Friday				
Saturday				

Week 12 Log

Dates: _____   to _____

Weight: _____   Resting pulse: _____

Week's Training

Day	Workout	Time	Distance	Pace
Sunday				
Monday				
Tuesday				
Wednesday				
Thursday				
Friday				
Saturday				

Short-Race Training: Week 13

Week's Program

Day	Workout (priority)	Duration	Pace	%V̇O₂max
Sunday	Steady state (2)	2/3 max+5 min	SWS	75-85%
Monday	Recovery (4)	1/4 max time	Easy	50-60%
Tuesday	Recovery (7)	1/4 max time	Easy	50-60%
Wednesday	Speed (3)	8 × 100 m	Strong	90-110%
Thursday	Recovery (5)	1/4 max time	Easy	50-60%
Friday	Recovery (6)	1/4 max time	Easy	50-60%
Saturday	Race (1)	Race	Goal pace	See intro

Week 13 Log

Dates: _____   to _____

Weight: _____   Resting pulse: _____

Week's Training

Day	Workout	Time	Distance	Pace
Sunday				
Monday				
Tuesday				
Wednesday				
Thursday				
Friday				
Saturday				

Half-Marathon Training

In all but its name, the half-marathon is a perfectly wonderful event. It is a true race, not a survival test (as the marathon can become), and its training isn't like taking on a second job (as marathon preparation sometimes seems). We only wish someone would rename the "half." It isn't a cut-rate version of a marathon, but a unique race with its own requirements and rewards.

This program, which also prepares you for other races in the 15K to 25K range, lasts 18 weeks, or a little over four months. Train four or five days each week if you're a casual racer, four to seven days if advanced. Priority numbers indicate the workouts' order of importance, with priority one being the most important, seven the least. When you run fewer days than seven, drop workouts from the highest number (7) downward. Determine appropriate lengths and paces of your runs from the tables in chapter 6. Remember from chapter 7 that SWS stands for somewhat strong. Then take this information and plug these figures into the training formulas supplied on the weekly log pages. Note that some formulas offer a range

The half-marathon is a unique race with its own requirements and rewards.

© The PhotoNews

of choices for duration of a run or number of repetitions. Base your selections on your current fitness level.

For tempo, interval, speed, and race-preparation workouts, add a warm-up of a 5- to 10-minute jog and 4 × 50-meter strides with slower ones of equal length (for example, 400 meters total with recovery jog/walks of 50 meters in between each). Also add a cool-down jog of 5 to 10 minutes.

Long training runs peak at 120 minutes (two hours) in these programs. If you reach that level, do not go higher.

Some weeks you get to choose between a long run or a tempo run. If you pick a long run, keep it at the same duration and intensity as the previous long one. The tempo run can be either a 40-minute run at SWS to strong effort or a 5K to 10K race for fun.

For all repetition-type workouts (strides, interval, speed, race-preparation), follow the faster segment with a slower one of equal length (for example, 4 × 400 meters with a 400-meter recovery jog/walk in between each).

For goal-pace runs, select a pace that corresponds to your $\dot{V}O_2$max plus four points. For example, a runner with a current reading of 50 has a goal-pace $\dot{V}O_2$max of 54.

After finishing the workout, record your results in the provided weekly log.

Half-Marathon Training: Week 1

Week's Program

Day	Workout (priority)	Duration	Pace	%$\dot{V}O_2$max
Sunday	Recovery (4)	1/2 max time	Easy	50-60%
Monday	Steady state (1)	2/3 max time	SWS	75-85%
Tuesday	Recovery (5)	1/2 max time	Easy	50-60%
Wednesday	Steady state (2)	2/3 max time	SWS	75-85%
Thursday	Recovery (6)	1/2 max time	Easy	50-60%
Friday	Steady state (3)	2/3 max time	SWS	75-85%
Saturday	Recovery (7)	1/2 max time	Easy	50-60%

Half-Marathon Training: Week 2

Week's Program

Day	Workout (priority)	Duration	Pace	%$\dot{V}O_2$max
Sunday	Long (1)	Max time	Moderate	60-70%
Monday	Recovery (4)	1/2 max time	Easy	50-60%
Tuesday	Recovery (6)	1/2 max time	Easy	50-60%
Wednesday	Race prep (3)	3 × 1 mile	Goal pace	see intro
Thursday	Recovery (5)	1/2 max	Easy	50-60%
Friday	Steady state (2)	2/3 max+1 min	SWS	75-85%
Saturday	Speed (7)	5 × 100 m	Strong	90-110%

Week 1 Log

Dates: _____   to _____

Weight: _____   Resting pulse: _____

Week's Training

Day	Workout	Time	Distance	Pace
Sunday				
Monday				
Tuesday				
Wednesday				
Thursday				
Friday				
Saturday				

Week 2 Log

Dates: _____   to _____

Weight: _____   Resting pulse: _____

Week's Training

Day	Workout	Time	Distance	Pace
Sunday				
Monday				
Tuesday				
Wednesday				
Thursday				
Friday				
Saturday				

Half-Marathon Training: Week 3

Week's Program

Day	Workout (priority)	Duration	Pace	%$\dot{V}O_2$max
Sunday	Long (1)	Max+5 min	Moderate	60-70%
Monday	Recovery (5)	1/2 max time	Easy	50-60%
Tuesday	Speed (4)	5 × 100 m	Strong	90-110%
Wednesday	Steady state (3)	2/3 max+2 min	SWS	75-85%
Thursday	Recovery (7)	1/2 max time	Easy	50-60%
Friday	Recovery (5)	1/2 max time	Easy	50-60%
Saturday	Tempo or long (2)	See intro	See intro	See intro

Half-Marathon Training: Week 4

Week's Program

Day	Workout (priority)	Duration	Pace	%$\dot{V}O_2$max
Sunday	Recovery (4)	1/2 max+2 min	Easy	50-60%
Monday	Steady state (1)	2/3 max+3 min	SWS	75-85%
Tuesday	Recovery (5)	1/2 max+2 min	Easy	50-60%
Wednesday	Steady state (2)	2/3 max+3 min	SWS	75-85%
Thursday	Recovery (6)	1/2 max+2 min	Easy	50-60%
Friday	Steady state (3)	2/3 max+3 min	SWS	75-85%
Saturday	Recovery (7)	1/2 max+2 min	Easy	50-60%

Week 3 Log

Dates: _____   to _____

Weight: _____   Resting pulse: _____

Week's Training

Day	Workout	Time	Distance	Pace
Sunday				
Monday				
Tuesday				
Wednesday				
Thursday				
Friday				
Saturday				

Week 4 Log

Dates: _____   to _____

Weight: _____   Resting pulse: _____

Week's Training

Day	Workout	Time	Distance	Pace
Sunday				
Monday				
Tuesday				
Wednesday				
Thursday				
Friday				
Saturday				

Half-Marathon Training: Week 5

Week's Program

Day	Workout (priority)	Duration	Pace	%$\dot{V}O_2$max
Sunday	Long (1)	Max+10 min	Moderate	60-70%
Monday	Recovery (4)	1/2 max+2 min	Easy	50-60%
Tuesday	Recovery (6)	1/2 max+2 min	Easy	50-60%
Wednesday	Race prep (3)	4 × 1 mile	Goal pace	See intro
Thursday	Recovery (7)	1/2 max+2 min	Easy	50-60%
Friday	Steady state (2)	2/3 max+3 min	SWS	75-85%
Saturday	Speed (7)	6 × 100 m	Strong	90-110%

Half-Marathon Training: Week 6

Week's Program

Day	Workout (priority)	Duration	Pace	%$\dot{V}O_2$max
Sunday	Long (1)	Max+15 min	Moderate	60-70%
Monday	Recovery (6)	1/2 max+2 min	Easy	50-60%
Tuesday	Speed (4)	6 × 100 m	Strong	90-110%
Wednesday	Steady state (3)	2/3 max+3 min	SWS	75-85%
Thursday	Recovery (7)	1/2 max+2 min	Easy	50-60%
Friday	Recovery (5)	1/4 max time	Easy	50-60%
Saturday	Tempo or long (2)	See note	See intro	See intro

Week 5 Log

Dates: _____ to _____

Weight: _____ Resting pulse: _____

Week's Training

Day	Workout	Time	Distance	Pace
Sunday				
Monday				
Tuesday				
Wednesday				
Thursday				
Friday				
Saturday				

Week 6 Log

Dates: _____ to _____

Weight: _____ Resting pulse: _____

Week's Training

Day	Workout	Time	Distance	Pace
Sunday				
Monday				
Tuesday				
Wednesday				
Thursday				
Friday				
Saturday				

Half-Marathon Training: Week 7

Week's Program

Day	Workout (priority)	Duration	Pace	%$\dot{V}O_2$max
Sunday	Recovery (4)	1/2 max+4 min	Easy	50-60%
Monday	Steady state (1)	2/3 max+6 min	SWS	75-85%
Tuesday	Recovery (5)	1/2 max+4 min	Easy	50-60%
Wednesday	Steady state (2)	2/3 max+6 min	SWS	75-85%
Thursday	Recovery (6)	1/2 max+4 min	Easy	50-60%
Friday	Steady state (3)	2/3 max+6 min	SWS	75-85%
Saturday	Recovery (7)	1/2 max+4 min	Easy	50-60%

Half-Marathon Training: Week 8

Week's Program

Day	Workout (priority)	Duration	Pace	%$\dot{V}O_2$max
Sunday	Long (1)	Max+20 min	Moderate	60-70%
Monday	Recovery (4)	1/2 max+4 min	Easy	50-60%
Tuesday	Recovery (6)	1/2 max+4 min	Easy	50-60%
Wednesday	Race prep (3)	5 × 1 mile	Goal pace	See intro
Thursday	Recovery (5)	1/2 max+4 min	Easy	50-60%
Friday	Steady state (2)	2/3 max+6 min	SWS	75-85%
Saturday	Speed (7)	6 × 150 m	Strong	90-110%

Week 7 Log

Dates: _____   to _____

Weight: _____   Resting pulse: _____

Week's Training

Day	Workout	Time	Distance	Pace
Sunday				
Monday				
Tuesday				
Wednesday				
Thursday				
Friday				
Saturday				

Week 8 Log

Dates: _____   to _____

Weight: _____   Resting pulse: _____

Week's Training

Day	Workout	Time	Distance	Pace
Sunday				
Monday				
Tuesday				
Wednesday				
Thursday				
Friday				
Saturday				

Half-Marathon Training: Week 9

Week's Program

Day	Workout (priority)	Duration	Pace	%$\dot{V}O_2$max
Sunday	Long (1)	Max+25 min	Moderate	60-70%
Monday	Recovery (6)	1/2 max+4 min	Easy	50-60%
Tuesday	Speed (4)	6 × 100 m	Strong	90-110%
Wednesday	Steady state (3)	2/3 max+6 min	SWS	75-85%
Thursday	Recovery (7)	1/2 max+4 min	Easy	50-60%
Friday	Steady state (5)	1/4 max time	Easy	50-60%
Saturday	Tempo or long (2)	See note	See intro	See intro

Half-Marathon Training: Week 10

Week's Program

Day	Workout (priority)	Duration	Pace	%$\dot{V}O_2$max
Sunday	Recovery (4)	1/2 max+6 min	Easy	50-60%
Monday	Steady state (1)	2/3 max+8 min	SWS	75-85%
Tuesday	Recovery (5)	1/2 max+6 min	Easy	50-60%
Wednesday	Steady state (2)	2/3 max+8 min	SWS	75-85%
Thursday	Recovery (6)	1/2 max+6 min	Easy	50-60%
Friday	Steady state (3)	2/3 max+8 min	SWS	75-85%
Saturday	Recovery (7)	1/2 max+6 min	Easy	50-60%

Week 9 Log

Dates: _____   to _____

Weight: _____   Resting pulse: _____

Week's Training

Day	Workout	Time	Distance	Pace
Sunday				
Monday				
Tuesday				
Wednesday				
Thursday				
Friday				
Saturday				

Week 10 Log

Dates: _____   to _____

Weight: _____   Resting pulse: _____

Week's Training

Day	Workout	Time	Distance	Pace
Sunday				
Monday				
Tuesday				
Wednesday				
Thursday				
Friday				
Saturday				

Half-Marathon Training: Week 11

Week's Program

Day	Workout (priority)	Duration	Pace	%$\dot{V}O_2$max
Sunday	Long (1)	Max+30 min	Moderate	60-70%
Monday	Recovery (4)	1/2 max+6 min	Easy	50-60%
Tuesday	Recovery (6)	1/2 max+6 min	Easy	50-60%
Wednesday	Race prep (3)	6 × 1 mile	Goal pace	See intro
Thursday	Recovery (5)	1/2 max+6 min	Easy	50-60%
Friday	Steady state (2)	2/3 max+6 min	SWS	75-85%
Saturday	Speed (7)	6 × 150 m	Strong	90-110%

Half-Marathon Training: Week 12

Week's Program

Day	Workout (priority)	Duration	Pace	%$\dot{V}O_2$max
Sunday	Long (1)	Max+35 min	Moderate	60-70%
Monday	Recovery (6)	1/2 max+6 min	Easy	50-60%
Tuesday	Speed (4)	6 × 100 m	Strong	75-85%
Wednesday	Steady state (3)	2/3 max+8 min	SWS	75-85%
Thursday	Recovery (7)	1/2 max+6 min	Easy	50-60%
Friday	Recovery (5)	1/4 max time	Easy	50-60%
Saturday	Tempo or long (2)	See note	See intro	See intro

Week 11 Log

Dates: _____   to _____

Weight: _____   Resting pulse: _____

Week's Training

Day	Workout	Time	Distance	Pace
Sunday				
Monday				
Tuesday				
Wednesday				
Thursday				
Friday				
Saturday				

Week 12 Log

Dates: _____   to _____

Weight: _____   Resting pulse: _____

Week's Training

Day	Workout	Time	Distance	Pace
Sunday				
Monday				
Tuesday				
Wednesday				
Thursday				
Friday				
Saturday				

Half-Marathon Training: Week 13

Week's Program

Day	Workout (priority)	Duration	Pace	%$\dot{V}O_2$max
Sunday	Recovery (4)	1/2 max+8 min	Easy	50-60%
Monday	Steady state (1)	2/3 max+10 min	SWS	75-85%
Tuesday	Recovery (5)	1/2 max+8 min	Easy	50-60%
Wednesday	Steady state (2)	2/3 max+10 min	SWS	75-85%
Thursday	Recovery (6)	1/2 max+8 min	Easy	50-60%
Friday	Steady state (3)	2/3 max+10 min	SWS	75-85%
Saturday	Recovery (7)	1/2 max+8 min	Easy	50-60%

Half-Marathon Training: Week 14

Week's Program

Day	Workout (priority)	Duration	Pace	%$\dot{V}O_2$max
Sunday	Long (1)	Max+40 min	Moderate	60-70%
Monday	Recovery (4)	1/2 max+8 min	Easy	50-60%
Tuesday	Recovery (6)	1/2 max+8 min	Easy	50-60%
Wednesday	Race prep (3)	7 × 1 mile	Goal pace	See intro
Thursday	Recovery (5)	1/2 max+8 min	Easy	50-60%
Friday	Steady state (2)	2/3 max+10 min	SWS	75-85%
Saturday	Interval (7)	5 × 200 m	Strong	90-110%

Week 13 Log

Dates: _____   to _____

Weight: _____   Resting pulse: _____

Week's Training

Day	Workout	Time	Distance	Pace
Sunday				
Monday				
Tuesday				
Wednesday				
Thursday				
Friday				
Saturday				

Week 14 Log

Dates: _____   to _____

Weight: _____   Resting pulse: _____

Week's Training

Day	Workout	Time	Distance	Pace
Sunday				
Monday				
Tuesday				
Wednesday				
Thursday				
Friday				
Saturday				

Half-Marathon Training: Week 15

Week's Program

Day	Workout (priority)	Duration	Pace	%$\dot{V}O_2$max
Sunday	Long (1)	Max+45 min	Moderate	60-70%
Monday	Recovery (6)	1/2 max+8 min	Easy	50-60%
Tuesday	Speed (4)	6 × 100 m	Strong	90-110%
Wednesday	Steady state (3)	2/3 max+10 min	SWS	75-85%
Thursday	Recovery (7)	1/2 max+8 min	Easy	50-60%
Friday	Recovery (5)	1/4 max time	Easy	50-60%
Saturday	Tempo or long (2)	See note	See intro	See intro

Half-Marathon Training: Week 16

Week's Program

Day	Workout (priority)	Duration	Pace	%$\dot{V}O_2$max
Sunday	Recovery (3)	1/2 max+4 min	Easy	50-60%
Monday	Recovery (6)	1/2 max+4 min	Easy	50-60%
Tuesday	Race prep (1)	6 × 1 mile	Goal pace	See intro
Wednesday	Recovery (4)	1/2 max+4 min	Easy	50-60%
Thursday	Race prep (2)	8 × 800 m	Goal pace	See intro
Friday	Recovery (5)	1/2 max+4 min	Easy	50-60%
Saturday	Recovery (7)	1/2 max+4 min	Easy	50-60%

Week 15 Log

Dates: _____   to _____

Weight: _____   Resting pulse: _____

Week's Training

Day	Workout	Time	Distance	Pace
Sunday				
Monday				
Tuesday				
Wednesday				
Thursday				
Friday				
Saturday				

Week 16 Log

Dates: _____   to _____

Weight: _____   Resting pulse: _____

Week's Training

Day	Workout	Time	Distance	Pace
Sunday				
Monday				
Tuesday				
Wednesday				
Thursday				
Friday				
Saturday				

Half-Marathon Training: Week 17

Week's Program

Day	Workout (priority)	Duration	Pace	%$\dot{V}O_2$max
Sunday	Long (1)	Max+30 min	Moderate	60-70%
Monday	Recovery (4)	1/2 max+4 min	Easy	50-60%
Tuesday	Interval (2)	12 × 400 m	Strong	90-110%
Wednesday	Recovery (5)	1/2 max+4 min	Easy	50-60%
Thursday	Race prep (3)	5 × 1 mile	Goal pace	See intro
Friday	Recovery (6)	1/2 max+4 min	Easy	50-60%
Saturday	Recovery (7)	1/2 max+4 min	Easy	50-60%

Half-Marathon Training: Week 18

Week's Program

Day	Workout (priority)	Duration	Pace	%$\dot{V}O_2$max
Sunday	Steady state (2)	2/3 max time	Moderate	60-70%
Monday	Recovery (4)	1/2 max+4 min	Easy	50-60%
Tuesday	Recovery (7)	1/2 max+4 min	Easy	50-60%
Wednesday	Speed (3)	6 × 100 m	Strong	90-110%
Thursday	Recovery (5)	1/4 max time	Easy	50-60%
Friday	Recovery (6)	1/4 max time	Easy	50-60%
Saturday	Race (1)	Half-marathon	Goal pace	See intro

Week 17 Log

Dates: _____ to _____

Weight: _____ Resting pulse: _____

Week's Training

Day	Workout	Time	Distance	Pace
Sunday				
Monday				
Tuesday				
Wednesday				
Thursday				
Friday				
Saturday				

Week 18 Log

Dates: _____ to _____

Weight: _____ Resting pulse: _____

Week's Training

Day	Workout	Time	Distance	Pace
Sunday				
Monday				
Tuesday				
Wednesday				
Thursday				
Friday				
Saturday				

14

Marathon Training

Marathons are hard work. They don't begin at the starting line but in the training that begins many months earlier. They take hours to run, and they end, not at the finish line, but with recovery that lasts for weeks. The difficulty of the marathon is one of its attractions, and the distance is covered by a half-million finishers a year in the United States alone.

This program, which also prepares you for other races 30K and longer, extends 26 weeks, or six months, or half a year. Train four to five days each week if you're a casual racer, four to seven days if advanced. Priority numbers indicate a workout's order of importance, with priority one being the most important, seven the least. When you run fewer days than seven, drop workouts from the highest number (7) downward. Determine appropriate lengths and paces of your runs from the tables in chapter 6. Remember from chapter 7 that SWS stands for somewhat strong. Then take this information and plug these figures into the training formulas supplied on the weekly log pages. Note that some formulas offer a range of choices for duration of a run or number of repetitions. Base your selections on your current fitness level.

The great challenge of the marathon attracts runners and spurs them on to meet their goals.

© Human Kinetics

For tempo, interval, speed, and race-preparation workouts, add a warm-up of a 5- to 10-minute jog and 4×50-meter strides with slower ones of equal length (for example, 400 meters total with recovery jog/walks of 50 meters in between each). Also add a cool-down jog of 5 to 10 minutes.

Some weeks you get to choose between a long run or a tempo run. If you pick a long run, keep it at the same duration and intensity as the previous long one. The tempo run can be either a 40-minute run at SWS to strong effort or a 5K to 10K race for fun.

For all repetition-type workouts (strides, interval, speed, race-preparation), follow the faster segment with a slower one of equal length (for example, 4×400 meters with a 400-meter recovery jog/walk in between each).

For goal-pace runs, select a pace that corresponds to your $\dot{V}O_2$max plus four points. For example, a runner with a current reading of 50 has a goal-pace $\dot{V}O_2$max of 54.

After finishing the workout, record your results in the weekly log provided here.

Marathon Training: Week 1

Week's Program

Day	Workout (priority)	Duration	Pace	%$\dot{V}O_2$max
Sunday	Recovery (4)	1/2 max time	Easy	50-60%
Monday	Steady state (1)	2/3 max time	SWS	75-85%
Tuesday	Recovery (5)	1/2 max time	Easy	50-60%
Wednesday	Steady state (2)	2/3 max time	SWS	75-85%
Thursday	Recovery (6)	1/2 max time	Easy	50-60%
Friday	Steady state (3)	2/3 max time	SWS	75-85%
Saturday	Recovery (7)	1/2 max time	Easy	50-60%

Marathon Training: Week 2

Week's Program

Day	Workout (priority)	Duration	Pace	%$\dot{V}O_2$max
Sunday	Long (1)	Max time	Moderate	60-70%
Monday	Recovery (4)	1/2 max time	Easy	50-60%
Tuesday	Recovery (6)	1/2 max time	Easy	50-60%
Wednesday	Race prep (3)	3 × 1 mile	Goal pace	see intro
Thursday	Recovery (5)	1/2 max	Easy	50-60%
Friday	Steady state (2)	2/3 max+1 min	SWS	75-85%
Saturday	Speed (7)	5 × 100 m	Strong	90-110%

Week 1 Log

Dates: _____   to _____

Weight: _____   Resting pulse: _____

Week's Training

Day	Workout	Time	Distance	Pace
Sunday				
Monday				
Tuesday				
Wednesday				
Thursday				
Friday				
Saturday				

Week 2 Log

Dates: _____   to _____

Weight: _____   Resting pulse: _____

Week's Training

Day	Workout	Time	Distance	Pace
Sunday				
Monday				
Tuesday				
Wednesday				
Thursday				
Friday				
Saturday				

Marathon Training: Week 3

Week's Program

Day	Workout (priority)	Duration	Pace	%$\dot{V}O_2$max
Sunday	Long (1)	Max+5 min	Moderate	60-70%
Monday	Recovery (5)	1/2 max time	Easy	50-60%
Tuesday	Speed (4)	5 × 100 m	Strong	90-110%
Wednesday	Steady state (3)	2/3 max+2 min	SWS	75-85%
Thursday	Recovery (7)	1/2 max time	Easy	50-60%
Friday	Recovery (5)	1/2 max time	Easy	50-60%
Saturday	Tempo or long (2)	See intro	See intro	See intro

Marathon Training: Week 4

Week's Program

Day	Workout (priority)	Duration	Pace	%$\dot{V}O_2$max
Sunday	Recovery (4)	1/2 max+2 min	Easy	50-60%
Monday	Steady state (1)	2/3 max+3 min	SWS	75-85%
Tuesday	Recovery (5)	1/2 max+2 min	Easy	50-60%
Wednesday	Steady state (2)	2/3 max+3 min	SWS	75-85%
Thursday	Recovery (6)	1/2 max+2 min	Easy	50-60%
Friday	Steady state (3)	2/3 max+3 min	SWS	75-85%
Saturday	Recovery (7)	1/2 max+2 min	Easy	50-60%

Week 3 Log

Dates: _____   to _____

Weight: _____   Resting pulse: _____

Week's Training

Day	Workout	Time	Distance	Pace
Sunday				
Monday				
Tuesday				
Wednesday				
Thursday				
Friday				
Saturday				

Week 4 Log

Dates: _____   to _____

Weight: _____   Resting pulse: _____

Week's Training

Day	Workout	Time	Distance	Pace
Sunday				
Monday				
Tuesday				
Wednesday				
Thursday				
Friday				
Saturday				

Marathon Training: Week 5

Week's Program

Day	Workout (priority)	Duration	Pace	%$\dot{V}O_2$max
Sunday	Long (1)	Max+10 min	Moderate	60-70%
Monday	Recovery (4)	1/2 max+2 min	Easy	50-60%
Tuesday	Recovery (6)	1/2 max+2 min	Easy	50-60%
Wednesday	Race prep (3)	4 × 1 mile	Goal pace	See intro
Thursday	Recovery (7)	1/2 max+2 min	Easy	50-60%
Friday	Steady state (2)	2/3 max+3 min	SWS	75-85%
Saturday	Speed (7)	6 × 100 m	Strong	90-110%

Marathon Training: Week 6

Week's Program

Day	Workout (priority)	Duration	Pace	%$\dot{V}O_2$max
Sunday	Long (1)	Max+15 min	Moderate	60-70%
Monday	Recovery (6)	1/2 max+2 min	Easy	50-60%
Tuesday	Speed (4)	6 × 100 m	Strong	90-110%
Wednesday	Steady state (3)	2/3 max+3 min	SWS	75-85%
Thursday	Recovery (7)	1/2 max+2 min	Easy	50-60%
Friday	Recovery (5)	1/4 max time	Easy	50-60%
Saturday	Tempo or long (2)	See note	See intro	See intro

Week 5 Log

Dates: _____   to _____

Weight: _____   Resting pulse: _____

Week's Training

Day	Workout	Time	Distance	Pace
Sunday				
Monday				
Tuesday				
Wednesday				
Thursday				
Friday				
Saturday				

Week 6 Log

Dates: _____   to _____

Weight: _____   Resting pulse: _____

Week's Training

Day	Workout	Time	Distance	Pace
Sunday				
Monday				
Tuesday				
Wednesday				
Thursday				
Friday				
Saturday				

Marathon Training: Week 7

Week's Program

Day	Workout (priority)	Duration	Pace	%$\dot{V}O_2$max
Sunday	Recovery (4)	1/2 max+4 min	Easy	50-60%
Monday	Steady state (1)	2/3 max+6 min	SWS	75-85%
Tuesday	Recovery (5)	1/2 max+4 min	Easy	50-60%
Wednesday	Steady state (2)	2/3 max+6 min	SWS	75-85%
Thursday	Recovery (6)	1/2 max+4 min	Easy	50-60%
Friday	Steady state (3)	2/3 max+6 min	SWS	75-85%
Saturday	Recovery (7)	1/2 max+4 min	Easy	50-60%

Marathon Training: Week 8

Week's Program

Day	Workout (priority)	Duration	Pace	%$\dot{V}O_2$max
Sunday	Long (1)	Max+20 min	Moderate	60-70%
Monday	Recovery (4)	1/2 max+4 min	Easy	50-60%
Tuesday	Recovery (6)	1/2 max+4 min	Easy	50-60%
Wednesday	Race prep (3)	5 × 1 mile	Goal pace	See intro
Thursday	Recovery (5)	1/2 max+4 min	Easy	50-60%
Friday	Steady state (2)	2/3 max+6 min	SWS	75-85%
Saturday	Speed (7)	6 × 150 m	Strong	90-110%

Week 7 Log

Dates: _____   to _____

Weight: _____   Resting pulse: _____

Week's Training

Day	Workout	Time	Distance	Pace
Sunday				
Monday				
Tuesday				
Wednesday				
Thursday				
Friday				
Saturday				

Week 8 Log

Dates: _____   to _____

Weight: _____   Resting pulse: _____

Week's Training

Day	Workout	Time	Distance	Pace
Sunday				
Monday				
Tuesday				
Wednesday				
Thursday				
Friday				
Saturday				

Marathon Training: Week 9

Week's Program

Day	Workout (priority)	Duration	Pace	%$\dot{V}O_2$max
Sunday	Long (1)	Max+25 min	Moderate	60-70%
Monday	Recovery (6)	1/2 max+4 min	Easy	50-60%
Tuesday	Speed (4)	6 × 100 m	Strong	90-110%
Wednesday	Steady state (3)	2/3 max+6 min	SWS	75-85%
Thursday	Recovery (7)	1/2 max+4 min	Easy	50-60%
Friday	Steady state (5)	1/4 max time	Easy	50-60%
Saturday	Tempo or long (2)	See intro	See intro	See intro

Marathon Training: Week 10

Week's Program

Day	Workout (priority)	Duration	Pace	%$\dot{V}O_2$max
Sunday	Recovery (4)	1/2 max+6 min	Easy	50-60%
Monday	Steady state (1)	2/3 max+8 min	SWS	75-85%
Tuesday	Recovery (5)	1/2 max+6 min	Easy	50-60%
Wednesday	Steady state (2)	2/3 max+8 min	SWS	75-85%
Thursday	Recovery (6)	1/2 max+6 min	Easy	50-60%
Friday	Steady state (3)	2/3 max+8 min	SWS	75-85%
Saturday	Recovery (7)	1/2 max+6 min	Easy	50-60%

Week 9 Log

Dates: _____   to _____

Weight: _____   Resting pulse: _____

Week's Training

Day	Workout	Time	Distance	Pace
Sunday				
Monday				
Tuesday				
Wednesday				
Thursday				
Friday				
Saturday				

Week 10 Log

Dates: _____   to _____

Weight: _____   Resting pulse: _____

Week's Training

Day	Workout	Time	Distance	Pace
Sunday				
Monday				
Tuesday				
Wednesday				
Thursday				
Friday				
Saturday				

Marathon Training: Week 11

Week's Program

Day	Workout (priority)	Duration	Pace	%$\dot{V}O_2$max
Sunday	Long (1)	Max+30 min	Moderate	60-70%
Monday	Recovery (4)	1/2 max+6 min	Easy	50-60%
Tuesday	Recovery (6)	1/2 max+6 min	Easy	50-60%
Wednesday	Race prep (3)	6 × 1 mile	Goal pace	See intro
Thursday	Recovery (5)	1/2 max+6 min	Easy	50-60%
Friday	Steady state (2)	2/3 max+6 min	SWS	75-85%
Saturday	Speed (7)	6 × 150 m	Strong	90-110%

Marathon Training: Week 12

Week's Program

Day	Workout (priority)	Duration	Pace	%$\dot{V}O_2$max
Sunday	Long (1)	Max+35 min	Moderate	60-70%
Monday	Recovery (6)	1/2 max+6 min	Easy	50-60%
Tuesday	Speed (4)	6 × 100 m	Strong	90-110%
Wednesday	Steady state (3)	2/3 max+8 min	SWS	75-85%
Thursday	Recovery (7)	1/2 max+6 min	Easy	50-60%
Friday	Recovery (5)	1/4 max time	Easy	50-60%
Saturday	Tempo or long (2)	See intro	See intro	See intro

Week 11 Log

Dates: _____   to _____

Weight: _____   Resting pulse: _____

Week's Training

Day	Workout	Time	Distance	Pace
Sunday				
Monday				
Tuesday				
Wednesday				
Thursday				
Friday				
Saturday				

Week 12 Log

Dates: _____ to _____

Weight: _____ Resting pulse: _____

Week's Training

Day	Workout	Time	Distance	Pace
Sunday				
Monday				
Tuesday				
Wednesday				
Thursday				
Friday				
Saturday				

Marathon Training: Week 13

Week's Program

Day	Workout (priority)	Duration	Pace	%$\dot{V}O_2$max
Sunday	Recovery (4)	1/2 max+8 min	Easy	50-60%
Monday	Steady state (1)	2/3 max+10 min	SWS	75-85%
Tuesday	Recovery (5)	1/2 max+8 min	Easy	50-60%
Wednesday	Steady state (2)	2/3 max+10 min	SWS	75-85%
Thursday	Recovery (6)	1/2 max+8 min	Easy	50-60%
Friday	Steady state (3)	2/3 max+10 min	SWS	75-85%
Saturday	Recovery (7)	1/2 max+8 min	Easy	50-60%

Marathon Training: Week 14

Week's Program

Day	Workout (priority)	Duration	Pace	%$\dot{V}O_2$max
Sunday	Long (1)	Max+40 min	Moderate	60-70%
Monday	Recovery (4)	1/2 max+8 min	Easy	50-60%
Tuesday	Recovery (6)	1/2 max+8 min	Easy	50-60%
Wednesday	Race prep (3)	7 × 1 mile	Goal pace	See intro
Thursday	Recovery (5)	1/2 max+8 min	Easy	50-60%
Friday	Steady state (2)	2/3 max+10 min	SWS	75-85%
Saturday	Interval (7)	5 × 200 m	Strong	90-110%

Week 13 Log

Dates: _____   to _____

Weight: _____   Resting pulse: _____

Week's Training

Day	Workout	Time	Distance	Pace
Sunday				
Monday				
Tuesday				
Wednesday				
Thursday				
Friday				
Saturday				

Week 14 Log

Dates: _____   to _____

Weight: _____   Resting pulse: _____

Week's Training

Day	Workout	Time	Distance	Pace
Sunday				
Monday				
Tuesday				
Wednesday				
Thursday				
Friday				
Saturday				

Marathon Training: Week 15

Week's Program

Day	Workout (priority)	Duration	Pace	%$\dot{V}O_2$max
Sunday	Long (1)	Max+45 min	Moderate	60-70%
Monday	Recovery (6)	1/2 max+8 min	Easy	50-60%
Tuesday	Speed (4)	6 × 100 m	Strong	90-110%
Wednesday	Steady state (3)	2/3 max+10 min	SWS	75-85%
Thursday	Recovery (7)	1/2 max+8 min	Easy	50-60%
Friday	Recovery (5)	1/4 max time	Easy	50-60%
Saturday	Tempo or long (2)	See intro	See intro	See intro

Marathon Training: Week 16

Week's Program

Day	Workout (priority)	Duration	Pace	%$\dot{V}O_2$max
Sunday	Recovery (4)	1/2 max+10 min	Easy	50-60%
Monday	Steady state (1)	2/3 max+12 min	SWS	75-85%
Tuesday	Recovery (5)	1/2 max+10 min	Easy	50-60%
Wednesday	Steady state (2)	1/2 max+12 min	SWS	75-85%
Thursday	Recovery (7)	1/2 max+10 min	Easy	50-60%
Friday	Steady state (3)	2/3 max+12 min	SWS	75-85%
Saturday	Recovery (7)	1/2 max+10 min	Easy	50-60%

Week 15 Log

Dates: _____   to _____

Weight: _____   Resting pulse: _____

Week's Training

Day	Workout	Time	Distance	Pace
Sunday				
Monday				
Tuesday				
Wednesday				
Thursday				
Friday				
Saturday				

Week 16 Log

Dates: _____   to _____

Weight: _____   Resting pulse: _____

Week's Training

Day	Workout	Time	Distance	Pace
Sunday				
Monday				
Tuesday				
Wednesday				
Thursday				
Friday				
Saturday				

Marathon Training: Week 17

Week's Program

Day	Workout (priority)	Duration	Pace	%$\dot{V}O_2$max
Sunday	Long (1)	Max+45 min	Moderate	60-70%
Monday	Recovery (4)	1/2 max+10 min	Easy	50-60%
Tuesday	Recovery (6)	1/2 max+10 min	Easy	50-60%
Wednesday	Race prep (3)	8 × 1 mile	Goal pace	See intro
Thursday	Recovery (5)	1/2 max+10 min	Easy	50-60%
Friday	Steady state (2)	2/3 max+12 min	SWS	75-85%
Saturday	Interval (7)	6 × 200 m	Strong	90-110%

Marathon Training: Week 18

Week's Program

Day	Workout (priority)	Duration	Pace	%$\dot{V}O_2$max
Sunday	Long (1)	Max+50 min	Moderate	60-70%
Monday	Recovery (6)	1/2 max+10 min	Easy	50-60%
Tuesday	Speed (4)	8 × 100 m	Strong	90-110%
Wednesday	Steady state (3)	2/3 max+12 min	SWS	75-85%
Thursday	Recovery (7)	1/2 max+10 min	Easy	50-60%
Friday	Recovery (5)	1/4 max time	Easy	50-60%
Saturday	Tempo or long (2)	See intro	See intro	See intro

Week 17 Log

Dates: _____ to _____

Weight: _____ Resting pulse: _____

Week's Training

Day	Workout	Time	Distance	Pace
Sunday				
Monday				
Tuesday				
Wednesday				
Thursday				
Friday				
Saturday				

Week 18 Log

Dates: _____ to _____

Weight: _____ Resting pulse: _____

Week's Training

Day	Workout	Time	Distance	Pace
Sunday				
Monday				
Tuesday				
Wednesday				
Thursday				
Friday				
Saturday				

Marathon Training: Week 19

Week's Program

Day	Workout (priority)	Duration	Pace	%$\dot{V}O_2$max
Sunday	Recovery (4)	1/2 max+12 min	Easy	50-60%
Monday	Steady state (1)	2/3 max+14 min	SWS	75-85%
Tuesday	Recovery (5)	1/2 max+12 min	Easy	50-60%
Wednesday	Steady state (2)	2/3 max+14 min	SWS	75-85%
Thursday	Recovery (6)	1/2 max+12 min	Easy	50-60%
Friday	Steady state (3)	2/3 max+14 min	SWS	75-85%
Saturday	Recovery (7)	1/2 max+12 min	Easy	50-60%

Marathon Training: Week 20

Week's Program

Day	Workout (priority)	Duration	Pace	%$\dot{V}O_2$max
Sunday	Long (1)	Max+55 min	Moderate	60-70%
Monday	Recovery (4)	1/2 max+12 min	Easy	50-60%
Tuesday	Recovery (6)	1/2 max+12 min	Easy	50-60%
Wednesday	Race prep (3)	4 × 2 miles	Goal pace	See intro
Thursday	Recovery (5)	1/2 max+12 min	Easy	50-60%
Friday	Steady state (2)	2/3 max+14 min	SWS	75-85%
Saturday	Interval (7)	6 × 200 m	Strong	90-110%

Week 19 Log

Dates: _____   to _____

Weight: _____   Resting pulse: _____

Week's Training

Day	Workout	Time	Distance	Pace
Sunday				
Monday				
Tuesday				
Wednesday				
Thursday				
Friday				
Saturday				

Week 20 Log

Dates: _____   to _____

Weight: _____   Resting pulse: _____

Week's Training

Day	Workout	Time	Distance	Pace
Sunday				
Monday				
Tuesday				
Wednesday				
Thursday				
Friday				
Saturday				

Marathon Training: Week 21

Week's Program

Day	Workout (priority)	Duration	Pace	%$\dot{V}O_2$max
Sunday	Long (1)	Max+60 min	Moderate	60-70%
Monday	Recovery (6)	1/2 max+12 min	Easy	50-60%
Tuesday	Speed (4)	8 × 100 m	Strong	90-110%
Wednesday	Steady state (3)	2/3 max+14 min	SWS	75-85%
Thursday	Recovery (7)	1/2 max+12 min	Easy	50-60%
Friday	Recovery (5)	1/4 max time	Easy	50-60%
Saturday	Tempo or long (2)	See intro	See intro	See intro

Marathon Training: Week 22

Week's Program

Day	Workout (priority)	Duration	Pace	%$\dot{V}O_2$max
Sunday	Recovery (4)	1/2 max+8 min	Easy	50-60%
Monday	Steady state (1)	2/3 max+8 min	SWS	75-85%
Tuesday	Recovery (5)	1/2 max+8 min	Easy	50-60%
Wednesday	Steady state (2)	2/3 max+8 min	SWS	75-85%
Thursday	Recovery (6)	1/2 max+8 min	Easy	50-60%
Friday	Steady state (3)	2/3 max+8 min	SWS	75-85%
Saturday	Recovery (7)	1/2 max+8 min	Easy	50-60%

Week 21 Log

Dates: _____ to _____

Weight: _____ Resting pulse: _____

Week's Training

Day	Workout	Time	Distance	Pace
Sunday				
Monday				
Tuesday				
Wednesday				
Thursday				
Friday				
Saturday				

Week 22 Log

Dates: _____ to _____

Weight: _____ Resting pulse: _____

Week's Training

Day	Workout	Time	Distance	Pace
Sunday				
Monday				
Tuesday				
Wednesday				
Thursday				
Friday				
Saturday				

Marathon Training: Week 23

Week's Program

Day	Workout (priority)	Duration	Pace	%$\dot{V}O_2$max
Sunday	Long (1)	Max+60 min	Moderate	60-70%
Monday	Recovery (4)	1/2 max+8 min	Easy	50-60%
Tuesday	Recovery (6)	1/2 max+8 min	Easy	50-60%
Wednesday	Race prep (3)	4 × 2 miles	Goal pace	See note
Thursday	Recovery (5)	1/2 max+8 min	Easy	50-60%
Friday	Steady state (2)	2/3 max+8 min	SWS	75-85%
Saturday	Interval (7)	6 × 200 m	Strong	90-110%

Marathon Training: Week 24

Week's Program

Day	Workout (priority)	Duration	Pace	%$\dot{V}O_2$max
Sunday	Recovery (3)	1/2 max+4 min	Easy	50-60%
Monday	Recovery (6)	1/2 max+4 min	Easy	50-60%
Tuesday	Race prep (1)	6 × 1 mile	Goal pace	See intro
Wednesday	Recovery (4)	1/2 max+4 min	Easy	50-60%
Thursday	Race prep (2)	8 × 800 m	Goal pace	See intro
Friday	Recovery (5)	1/2 max+4 min	Easy	50-60%
Saturday	Recovery (7)	1/2 max+4 min	Easy	50-60%

Week 23 Log

Dates: _____   to _____

Weight: _____   Resting pulse: _____

Week's Training

Day	Workout	Time	Distance	Pace
Sunday				
Monday				
Tuesday				
Wednesday				
Thursday				
Friday				
Saturday				

Week 24 Log

Dates: _____   to _____

Weight: _____   Resting pulse: _____

Week's Training

Day	Workout	Time	Distance	Pace
Sunday				
Monday				
Tuesday				
Wednesday				
Thursday				
Friday				
Saturday				

Marathon Training: Week 25

Week's Program

Day	Workout (priority)	Duration	Pace	%$\dot{V}O_2$max
Sunday	Long (1)	Max+30 min	Moderate	60-70%
Monday	Recovery (4)	1/2 max+4 min	Easy	50-60%
Tuesday	Interval (2)	12 × 400 m	Strong	90-110%
Wednesday	Recovery (5)	1/2 max+4 min	Easy	50-60%
Thursday	Race prep (3)	3 × 1 mile	Goal pace	See intro
Friday	Recovery (6)	1/2 max time	Easy	50-60%
Saturday	Recovery (7)	1/2 max time	Easy	50-60%

Marathon Training: Week 26

Week's Program

Day	Workout (priority)	Duration	Pace	%$\dot{V}O_2$max
Sunday	Steady state (2)	2/3 max time	Moderate	60-70%
Monday	Recovery (4)	1/2 max time	Easy	50-60%
Tuesday	Recovery (7)	1/2 max time	Easy	50-60%
Wednesday	Speed (3)	6 × 100 m	Strong	90-110%
Thursday	Recovery (5)	1/4 max time	Easy	50-60%
Friday	Recovery (6)	1/4 max time	Easy	50-60%
Saturday	Race (1)	Marathon	Goal pace	See intro

Week 25 Log

Dates: _____   to _____

Weight: _____   Resting pulse: _____

Week's Training

Day	Workout	Time	Distance	Pace
Sunday				
Monday				
Tuesday				
Wednesday				
Thursday				
Friday				
Saturday				

Week 26 Log

Dates: _____   to _____

Weight: _____   Resting pulse: _____

Week's Training

Day	Workout	Time	Distance	Pace
Sunday				
Monday				
Tuesday				
Wednesday				
Thursday				
Friday				
Saturday				

Index

Note: The italicized *f* and *t* following page numbers refer to figures and tables, respectively.

About the Authors

Richard L. Brown, PhD, is a veteran coach and an exercise physiologist. His career began in 1963 as a three-sport coach at Bullis Preparatory School in Maryland. It continued at the United States Naval Academy, then at Mt. Blue High School in Maryland, and with the Athletics West track team as an exercise physiologist and director. In 1983, Brown was head coach of the U.S. world championship cross-country team, and he's been coaching independently ever since.

He has also served as a personal coach to an impressive list of world-class athletes, including Mary Decker Slaney, Suzy Favor Hamilton, and Vicki Huber. He is one of the few coaches to have coached athletes in the Summer and Winter Olympic Games and the Paralympics. He has coached athletes in each of the last five Olympic Games (1984, 1988, 1992, 1996, and 2000).

Brown earned his PhD in exercise and movement sciences from the University of Oregon in 1992. He currently lives in Coburg, Oregon.

Joe Henderson combined his passion for running with his natural talent for writing and became one of the most prolific running writers on the planet. Although Henderson never accomplished his first career goal of becoming a high school or college running coach, through his advice in hundreds of magazines and books and in frequent speeches to running groups, he has indirectly coached thousands of runners.

Henderson was born in Illinois in 1943 and grew up in Iowa, where he began running at age 14. After graduating from Drake University in Des Moines, he began his work in running journalism at *Track & Field News*. Today he continues as a columnist with *Runner's World* and as the publisher of the newsletter *Running Commentary.* He has authored or coauthored 24 books including the best-selling *Marathon Training* as well as four others from Human Kinetics—*Best Runs, Better Runs, Coaching Cross Country Successfully,* and *Running 101.*

Henderson has twice been named Journalist of the Year by the Road Runners Club of America. He is also a member of the Club's Hall of Fame. Henderson lives in Eugene, Oregon, with his wife, Barbara Shaw.

*You'll find
other outstanding
running resources at*

www.HumanKinetics.com

In the U.S. call

800-747-4457

Australia 08 8277 1555
Canada 800-465-7301
Europe .... +44 (0) 113 255 5665
New Zealand 09-523-3462

HUMAN KINETICS
The Premier Publisher in Sports and Fitness
P.O. Box 5076 • Champaign, IL 61825-5076 USA